just-see
PARIS

CONTENTS

Published by Thomas Cook Publishing
PO Box 227, Thorpe Wood
Peterborough PE3 6PU
United Kingdom

E–mail: books@thomascook.com

Text: © The Thomas Cook Group Ltd 2000
Maps: © The Thomas Cook Group Ltd 2000
Transport map: © TCS 2000

ISBN 1 841570 397

Distributed in the United States of America by the Globe Pequot Press,
PO Box 480, Guilford, Connecticut 06437, USA.

Distributed in Canada by Whitecap Books, 351 Lynn Avenue,
North Vancouver, British Columbia, Canada V7J 2C4.

Distributed in Australia and New Zealand by Peribo Pty Limited,
58 Beaumont Road, Mt Kuring-Gai, NSW, 2080, Australia.

Publisher: Stephen York
Commissioning Editor: Deborah Parker
Map Editor: Bernard Horton

Series Editor: Christopher Catling

Written and researched by: Mike Gerrard

Cover photograph: Chris Fairclough

must-see PARIS

MIKE GERRARD

Getting to know Paris

Discovering Paris

Everyone knows Paris, even those who have never been there. Whether it be for its fashion, its food or just the Eiffel Tower, the city lodges itself in everyone's mind. It is one of the world's great cities, like New York and Hong Kong – cities so uniquely themselves that they do not disappoint the visitor who discovers them to be exactly as they'd imagined – only more so.

Paris has such depths, and its citizens are so contradictory, that it would take forever to unravel its mysteries. On a weekend visit anyone can be forgiven for playing the tourist, seeing the sights, because when Paris works its magic you know you will be back for more, especially as the Eurostar service now makes travel there so easy. It also makes it easier for Parisians to visit London and discover that there are other stylish cities, so the cross-cultural influence can only benefit both.

Toujours la politesse

One benefit will be to nail the old cliché that is repeated by British people constantly, that Parisians are rude. This is manifestly untrue. Parisians, like all French people, are polite, but the visitor has to return the politeness. Start every conversation with a cheery *Bonjour!*, even when simply buying your Métro tickets, and all will be well. Address everyone – even the buskers and beggars on the Métro – as *Monsieur* or *Madame*. Remember the old remark that when you are in a foreign country, *you* are the one with the strange customs and peculiar habits.

The world's most beautiful city

And what a surface! It sometimes seems in Paris that every building is beautiful, every street elegantly designed. Only Prague can possibly compete. Not even the retreating Nazis could bring themselves to destroy the City of Light. If some Parisians are arrogant, then they have much to be arrogant about. As one Parisian observed: 'Every French person from outside Paris will tell you it is the most beautiful city in the world. They just think it's wasted on the Parisians, whom they don't like simply because they live here and they know it.'

Past glories

Any arrogance is excusable, as the world's eyes so frequently focus on Paris. Democracy may have been born in ancient Athens but it was the French Revolution that began a more democratic modern world. Another defining era was the 1960s, when Parisian students took centre stage and thought

they were storming the Bastille all over again. Paris is also the city of starving artists and American writers – Hemingway, Picasso, Oscar Wilde, Rodin, Scott Fitzgerald, Toulouse-Lautrec, Edmund White. It is the city of romance, the city of sex, the city of *haute couture* and *haute cuisine*, the city of outrage and protest, the city of art. Indeed, for many people it is simply *the* city.

> " *Either that wallpaper goes, or I do.* "
>
> **The alleged last words of Oscar Wilde as he lay dying in Paris**

A day in the life of Paris

It sometimes seems as if everyone is on holiday in Paris – shopping, visiting museums and galleries, eating, drinking, talking in cafés – and that's truer here than in most cities, as the Parisians do know how to enjoy life. And who wouldn't, when you can walk down any street and pass half a dozen intriguing-looking restaurants, bistros or brasseries, and gaze into shop windows with glistening displays of patisseries – dark chocolate, plump strawberries, bulging apricots?

You may not see many berets in Paris – though a few older men still wear them – but there is no more truly French sight than seeing someone walking through the street with a baguette under their arm. The end of the bread will probably be nibbled, as it's traditional that you have to eat this before you get it home. And you will see lovers in the streets and in the Métro, gazing longingly into each other's eyes, arms around each other, sometimes engaging in passionate kisses, oblivious of the people around them.

The fashion

Paris is the fashion capital of the world, and you'll certainly know it when you walk round, especially in one of 'the' streets, like the swish Rue du Faubourg St-Honoré, where women in winter wear furs so thick it's quite obvious the concept of animal rights has never crossed their mind. Such women are equally likely to be seen walking alongside – or carrying – the latest fashionable dog, and if there is one blot on the Paris landscape it is the amount of dog dirt that litters its streets. It disgraces the loveliest city in the world, and remains a problem despite all attempts to deal with it. Some owners are conscientious and use their pooper-scoopers, but you can unfortunately see with your own eyes that they are in the minority – and your eyes need to be constantly vigilant. Although Britain is said to be a nation of animal lovers, it can still come as a shock to visit Paris and find dogs in shops, in supermarkets and even in restaurants, sometimes popped onto a cushion on a seat to be fed titbits by the owner.

> " The beret never used to be the mark of a Frenchman; until 1923 it was Basque, and worn only in the Pyrenees region. Then suddenly it was adopted as a French fashion, becoming almost a national uniform by 1932, when twenty-three million were manufactured, virtually one for every Frenchman. But the fashion was almost as suddenly abandoned in the 1950s. "
>
> **Theodore Zeldin, *The French*
> (Collins, 1983)**

Markets and movies

There is even a market for dogs, but then there are markets for most things: stamps, books, flowers and of course innumerable food markets. When Parisians are not eating food they are shopping for it. And when not doing that they do enjoy the many fine galleries and museums that surround them, where the packed crowds are not only tourists. They are great cinema-goers too, and a typical issue of the weekly entertainment 'bible', *Pariscope*, contains more pages on the cinema than any other subject – almost a third of its pages are given over to listing the 300 or so films that can be seen in Paris every week. From croissants in the morning to popcorn at night, the Parisians indulge themselves in their city just as much as the visitors do.

Yesterday and tomorrow

Why Paris? Because a tribe of Celts called the Parisii moved from further east and settled on the Île de la Cité, creating a little fishing village on this island in the Seine in about 250 BC. They weren't the first people in Paris, as Neolithic evidence shows, but they gave the place its name.

Later the Romans came and gave France one of its most popular exports: Asterix. Christianity came with St Denis from Athens in the 3rd century AD, though his over-enthusiastic tirades against paganism, which involved destroying statues, resulted in him being beheaded with two of his acolytes on top of the highest hill in the area, which became known as Mons Martyrum, the Mount of the Martyrs (now Montmartre). Ironically the name of St Denis lives on in, amongst other places, Rue St-Denis – a rather unsaintly street these days.

Rulers and the power of the people

There followed various rulers, including the memorable such as Charlemagne, and the ones the French would rather forget – like the British, from 1420–36. A name that resonates down the centuries is Cardinal Richelieu, the power behind the throne of the under-age Louis XIII and responsible for such buildings as the Palais Royal and the Sorbonne. Those two places reflect two of the biggest events in French history: the storming of the Bastille on 14 July 1789 and the students who manned the barricades in May 1968. The latter might seem minor compared to the former, but it certainly frightened the French bourgeoisie and reminded governments everywhere of 'the power of the people'.

Today's political leaders

We owe much of the beauty of today's Paris to two French leaders who were politically poles apart: the right-wing Georges Pompidou and the left-wing François Mitterand. It was the right-winger who created the avant-garde Centre Beaubourg, or Pompidou Centre, or the left-winger who lavished attention and money on Paris's grand old buildings, cleaning them up in a campaign that provoked great controversy. After all, hadn't Notre-Dame always been black? It was also Mitterand who initiated one of Paris's most debated modern buildings: the glass pyramid outside the Louvre. Like Paris itself, the pyramid is stylish, contentious and cannot be ignored.

Tomorrow

Never content to bask in its existing beauty, Paris is like a woman who must have a new outfit for each new occasion. By the time this book appears, transformations will have been made (though where they are known about they are indicated in the text). The Orangerie is being renovated, so that the whole building can do justice to its magnificent and huge Monet paintings of water-lilies. The Centre Beaubourg is partly closed for renovation – though there are those who say it always *did* look like a building site. While it is being worked on, some of its collection of modern art is on display at the Palais de Tokyo. It will reopen on 31 December 1999 with new multimedia areas, a major exhibition on *Time* for the Millennium, and a revamped modern art display.

For the Millennium the Louvre is also opening a new wing to display never-before-seen primitive arts from Africa, Asia, America, India and the Pacific Ocean. There are countless other events planned, including turning the streets that lead into the Arc de Triomphe into one enormous illuminated clock face to count down the last few hours of 1999 using laser beams, while beams from other high buildings will illuminate what is planned to be the world's biggest clock. Paris may never seem to change, yet time never stands still there either.

People and places

Love them or hate them, you can seldom ignore the politicians of Paris. It's hardly surprising from the nation which produced Napoléon, and, more recently, the resolute General de Gaulle.

But what often sets French leaders apart from their counterparts in other countries is that they care passionately about Paris, and the city you see as you walk around does owe a great deal to them. The 1980s were electric years, with the left-wing Mitterand ruling the country and the right-wing Jacques Chirac the mayor of Paris. Sparks flew but old monuments were cleaned and striking new ones created. When Chirac took over as President of France in 1995, it was a short-lived reign during a period of social strife. An early general election in May 1997 ousted Chirac and brought in Lionel Jospin, in charge of a Socialist coalition which was a precursor of Tony Blair's success in Britain 12 months later.

The land in which chefs are kings

One of the most recent French chefs to make a name for himself is Christian Constant, who owes his own success in part to the recession of the early 1990s. He was chef at the Hôtel Crillon and saw that many of the expense-account lunches which kept the restaurant scene thriving were being cancelled. He started a trend for simpler places, in less fashionable areas where rents were cheap, the aim being to put together innovative menus using fresh local produce where people could dine for under 200 francs – preferably under 150. Most were chef-owned, and it was important for the chef actually to do the cooking and not merely oversee the kitchen. Many of the chefs worked under Constant, and there are now about 20–25 such places, including Au C'Amelot, L'Épi Dupin and Le Villaret. Constant has now bucked his own trend by opening Le Violon d'Ingres, where you're looking at a bill of at least 350 francs.

Fashion and its dedicated followers

Paris always was, still is, and seemingly always will be, the world centre of fashion. Which other city can boast so many household names like Coco Chanel, Christian Dior and Yves Saint-Laurent – who remains the superstar of the scene, despite the arrival of Young Turks like the Englishman John Galliano, the flamboyant Christian Lacroix and the outrageous flair of Jean-Paul Gaultier. With foreign names such as Vivienne Westwood, Issey Miyake, Kenzo and Armani all having showcase outlets in Paris, there remains no doubt about its supremacy. The world's eyes are on the city during its fashion weeks in January and July (for the *haute couture*) and March and October (for *prêt-à-porter*). Even if you can only afford to window-shop – what windows!

Film, photography and the arts

The Arts are almost like a blood that pulses through the veins of Paris, without which the city would die. It's been home to great photographers such as Man Ray, Robert Doisneau and perhaps the greatest of them all, Henri Cartier-Bresson, who still lives in the city today. Curiously it has never produced the wealth of rock musicians in the way that, say, London and New York have, yet if you threw a net over a typical city block, you'd very likely catch yourself one writer, three artists and a well-known movie star or director.

> " If you want to establish an international presence you can't do so from New York. You need the consecration of Paris. "
>
> **Oscar De La Renta, fashion designer, *International Herald Tribune*, 26 Feb 1991**

Paris-born Catherine Deneuve, who still lives in St-Germain, has led the kind of life the French expect their film stars to lead, having been married to the archetypal 'Swinging Sixties' photographer David Bailey, and having children by the movie director Roger Vadim and the Italian star Marcello Mastroianni. Her early successes included *Les Parapluies de Cherbourg*, *Repulsion* and *Belle de Jour*.

Getting around

RER

The RER is the express rail service that crosses Paris and links the centre with the outer suburbs. RER lines are referred to by a combination of letter and number, such as A3 or B4, and if travelling into the suburbs you need to make sure you take the right branch line. The service runs from 0530 to 2400.

Métro

Paris has the biggest and most efficient Métro system in the world, and also one of the cheapest in the western world. The Métro is also simple and logical. Lines are colour-coded and also have a number. All you need to know is the number of your line and the name of the end station in the direction you wish to travel. Follow signs for that number and name, and you will reach the platform you need. Trains run every few minutes.

Tickets can be bought individually or more economically in a carnet of ten tickets (*and see other options under* **Travel passes** *below*). Put your ticket into the entry gate and retain it for the duration of your journey. One ticket covers one journey, no matter how long or short, or whether you switch to the RER part-way through. You discard the ticket after the final exit gates. The Métro runs from 0530 to 0045.

Buses

The same tickets can be used on the bus network, but for longer journeys you should check with the driver as they may require two tickets. Get a map of the bus routes from the Métro station or tourist office, which shows which numbers go where. Again, the system is clear and logical. Each bus stop has a list of the bus numbers which stop there, the other stops on each route and the times of the first and last buses (the buses generally operate from roughly 0630 to 2100). Each bus also has a map of its route inside, and newer buses announce the name of the next stop as you approach it.

Taxis

Parisian taxis are not basically expensive, though fares can mount up when the traffic is heavy. There is the usual caution to make sure the meter is switched on. The white light on the roof means the cab is free, the orange light beneath it means it isn't. Taxi ranks are more common than in London, and it's usually advisable to ask for the nearest one as flagging down taxis in the street is not as common – and not as easy given the way the French drive. Allow for a tip of 10–20 per cent, though tipping is not compulsory.

River trips

Seeing Paris from the Seine on one of the *bateaux-mouches* which sail up and down the river gives a good view of many of its finest buildings. These tours, with multi-lingual commentaries, are a good option on a cold or wet day with their sheltered seating, and night-time dinner cruises are popular. The views of the floodlit buildings are usually better than the food provided. Daytime cruises generally last about an hour. Different companies leave from different points along the river, including the original Bateaux-

or *tabacs* (tobacconists) though you will need a passport photo. The various day passes can be obtained from Métro stations, where the current rates will be displayed enabling you to work out which will be the most economical for you. Carnets are generally better value unless you plan to do a great many Métro journeys each day.

Guided tours

As well as by boat, you can tour Paris by coach, on foot or even on bicycle, with an impressive range of tours to choose from. Conventional coach tours of the sights are run by Cityrama

Mouches company (*tel: 40 76 99 99 for information, 42 25 96 10 for reservations*), Bateaux-Parisiens (*tel: 47 05 50 00*), Vedettes Tour Eiffel (*tel: 45 05 50 00*), Les Vedettes de Paris (*tel: 47 05 71 29*) and Les Vedettes du Pont Neuf (*tel: 46 33 98 38*).

Travel passes

In addition to buying a carnet of ten tickets at a discount, you can buy passes for one, three or five days, or a Carte Orange valid for a week. The week always ends on Sunday evening, no matter when you buy this card, which you can get from Métro stations

(*tel: 44 55 61 00*) and Paris Vision (*tel: [08] 00 03 02 14*). Rather more imaginative are themed walking tours such as the Chic Promenade for shopaholics (*tel: 43 80 35 35*) or the Promenades Gourmandes for food and wine lovers (*tel: 48 04 56 84*). For cycle rental and/or guided tours, contact Paris-Vélo (*tel: 43 37 59 22*), Paris by Cycle (*tel: 42 63 36 63 or 40 47 08 04*), Mountain Bike Trip (*tel: 48 42 57 87*) or Paris à Vélo (*tel: 48 87 60 01*), which does bike tours at dawn, by night, around the tourist sights and to the lesser-known quarters.

Don't miss

✓✓1 The Louvre

The largest palace in Europe contains the best art collection in the world. It is breathtaking, but attempting it all in a single visit is likely to leave you breathless and foot-sore. **Pages 146–149**

✓✓2 Eiffel Tower

Paris's unique city symbol dominates the skyline, and as corny as it sounds, no visit is complete without a journey to the top. Spend a little time in Paris and the tower on the skyline starts to become an old friend. **Pages 22–23**

3 Musée d'Orsay

The second great art museum in the world's art capital. Many prefer it to the Louvre for its light, its space, its layout and of course its incomparable collection of Impressionists. If only all cities could convert their old railway stations with such *élan*. **Pages 40–41**

✓✓4 Arc de Triomphe

Bright and quite grand, this Napoleonic arch dominates the top of the Champs-Élysées and all the other streets which run off it. It is typically Parisian, combining grace and grandeur, self-importance and beauty – and cannot be ignored. **Pages 156–157**

✓✓5 Notre-Dame

One of the world's great cathedrals is built on the island in the Seine where Paris was born. It manages to encompass both sublime stained glass and gruesome gargoyles within its architectural variety. Even without Victor Hugo's 'Hunchback' adding to its fame, it would be an essential visit of any trip. **Pages 76–77**

✓✓ 6 Sacré-Coeur

Not all Parisians love the white cathedral on top of the hill of Montmartre, but the rooftop views from its steps are hard to beat. Whether you go the whole tourist hog and have your portrait painted by one of the nearby street artists is entirely up to you. **Pages 132–133**

7 Picasso Museum (Musée Picasso)

A monument to a monumental artistic talent, even non-fans might be turned into reluctant admirers of the Spanish genius's breadth of ability. He was an artist who could do anything, so what he chose to do with his gift is fascinating. **Pages 96–97**

8 Rodin Museum (Musée Rodin)

The best work of one of the world's best sculptors – including *The Kiss* and *The Thinker* – displayed inside and outside the home in which he died. Many of the pieces are here because the artist paid his rent with them. **Pages 30–31**

9 Centre Beaubourg (Pompidou Centre)

Great monument or great monstrosity? Well, almost eight million people a year come to see for themselves, making it the world's most-visited cultural site. **Pages 92–93**

10 Place des Vosges

At the other Parisian extreme from Pompidou brashness is this graceful 17th-century square framed by four rows of arcades. It is not a precious place, though, as its central gardens attract local children who play there and the old folk who watch them and remember. **Pages 100–101**

The Eiffel Tower and Les Invalides

Which first-time visitor to Paris doesn't head for the Eiffel Tower? But don't waste this first visit by popping up out of the ground at the nearest Métro. Get a sense of the structure's – and the city's – splendour by starting in the Trocadéro Gardens and approaching the tower by strolling over the Seine. And after the tower? Take a walk through the area of Les Invalides, to the east – one of the grander areas south of the river – ending up at the golden dome of the Hôtel des Invalides itself – not so much grand as grandiose, as you would expect from the building housing Napoléon's tomb.

THE EIFFEL TOWER AND LES INVALIDES

Getting there: **Métro:** For the Eiffel Tower head for Trocadéro first, unless the weather is foul. If it is, then go to Bir-Hakeim or École Militaire. Marenne is convenient for both the Hôtel des Invalides and the Musée Rodin. **RER:** For the tower take the RER to Champ de Mars Tour Eiffel. **Bus:** For the tower, use the 42, 69, 72, 82 or 87; for the Hôtel des Invalides and the Musée Rodin, 28, 49, 69, 82, 92.

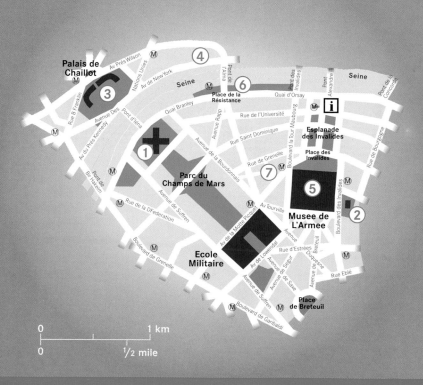

① The Eiffel Tower

Impossible to ignore, so why try? Dizzying views from the top but lengthy queues to get up there, so set off early to beat the crowds. Just hope you can beat the clouds too.
Pages 22–23

② You must see the Musée Rodin

Rodin is one of the many artists who lived in Paris and who can justifiably be called a genius in his field. Stand in front of *The Kiss* or gaze at *The Thinker* and you will know why.
Pages 30–31

③ Stroll through the Trocadéro Gardens

The gardens aren't huge but give a fabulous view across the Seine to the Eiffel Tower, and are a social focal point on a Sunday morning especially. If the sun is shining, the sky is blue and the fountains are playing, the whole effect is splendid. **Pages 24–25**

④ Visit the Musée d'Art Moderne de la Ville de Paris

Yet another excellent art collection – not the biggest, though it does contain the biggest painting in the world.
Pages 26–27

⑤ See Napoléon's tomb

You may or may not care for the style of the chapel in the Hôtel des Invalides, but there is a great feeling of history when you gaze down at the coffins – there are seven layered inside each other – containing the great man's mortal remains. **Pages 28–29**

⑥ Tour the sewers

A tourist attraction that caught everyone by surprise – who would have thought there'd be such an interest in getting a glimpse beneath the Parisian streets? But it's a great little expedition, not glossing over the problems involved in clearing away the sewerage of a huge city.
Pages 34–35

⑦ Shop in the market in Rue Cler

Paris is swamped with street markets, but this is something special – one of the most upmarket markets there is. Head here on a Saturday morning if you want to stock up on exclusive goodies for home, but take plenty of francs with you. **Page 31**

> " *For centuries the city's sewage ended up in the Seine, which also provided some of its drinking water. Not a good idea, concluded Napoleon, who ordered construction of the first underground sewage canals to take the waste away from the river. By 1850 there were already 100 miles of canals.* "

Alan Riding, 'The Sights Beneath the Sidewalks', *New York Times*

Tourist information

There is a tourist information office at the Eiffel Tower from May to September. *Champ de Mars.*
Tel: 45 51 22 15. Open daily.

The Eiffel Tower (La Tour Eiffel)

The Eiffel Tower was the tallest building in the world when it was constructed in the 1880s, and was built by over 300 workers to commemorate the centenary of the storming of the Bastille. It was opened for the 1889 International Exhibition of Paris, but the tower itself was almost stormed by protesters. Then 20 years later, when its planning permission expired in 1909, it was almost torn down. It was saved because its great height made it vital to the booming radio telegraphy industry.

Its designer, Gustave Eiffel (1832–1923), was the winner from among 700 entries in a competition to design a structure to commemorate the Bastille storming, and we can only be grateful that one of the other entries wasn't chosen: a giant guillotine. Eiffel jokingly referred to it as a 300m flagpole, but many others were less kind, calling it a Tower of Babel. The writer Guy de Maupassant said he liked to have lunch there because it was the only place in Paris where he didn't have to look at it. History has been rather more approving and a bust of Eiffel stands near the foot of the north corner.

Vital statistics

Work began in 1884, the bulk was done in 1887–9 (including the use of two-and-a-half million rivets, give or take a few), and its final height was exactly 300m, or 984ft. Since then the height has been increased by placing TV transmitters on the top, so now it stands at 320.75m (1051ft). Some days it stands even higher, as in the heat it expands by up to 15cm

A lick of paint

It takes a team of 25 painters 18 months to give a new lick of paint to the Eiffel Tower – and the 'lick' requires about 50 tons of paint. Then they wait seven years and start again. For the count-down to the Millennium, a huge digital display shows the number of days left till the end of the century.

(6in). The top hardly sways at all – by no more than 12cm (4.5in) on even the windiest days – no doubt helped by the fact that the tower weighs in at about 7000 tons (in fact it is kept stable by the complex criss-cross network of girders in Eiffel's design). As well as being used for radio and TV transmissions, the top contains a meteorological station and aircraft navigation equipment. It is said that on the proverbial clear day you can see not quite forever but for about 70km (45 miles).

Going up

Visitors can go as high as the third level of the tower, which is almost at the very top. You can reach the first level by either taking one of the lifts or climbing 360 steps. If that doesn't tire you, you can continue to climb a further 700 steps to the second level, or take the lift. At this point you can only take the lift to the very top, where there is space for up to 800 people. Even so, the top gets crowded and the queues for the lifts can wind for quite a way, so the best time to visit is first thing in the morning before too many crowds and coach parties arrive, or in the evening when most people are busy doing other things.

Getting there: In the Parc du Champ de Mars on Avenue Gustave Eiffel, open daily 0930–2300.

" *Nowhere is one more alone than in Paris … and yet surrounded by crowds. Nowhere is one more likely to incur greater ridicule. And no visit is more essential.* "

Marguerite Duras, 'Tourists in Paris' in *France-Observateur* (Paris, 1957; reproduced in *Outside: Selected Writings*, 1984)

The Palais de Chaillot and Trocadéro Gardens

*Like the Palais de Tokyo (see pages 26–27), the **Palais de Chaillot** was built for the Paris World Exhibition of 1937, situated across the Seine from the Eiffel Tower. Undoubtedly the best views of the tower are from the walls behind the Palais, where steps drop away to the small terraces of the **Jardins du Trocadéro (Trocadéro Gardens)**.*

The steps here are a hive of activity most days, as tour buses disgorge visitors for the view of the tower – but especially so on Sundays, when many Parisians also join the throngs of mostly North African vendors selling carvings, hats, paintings and general souvenirs.

> **"** *We'll always have Paris.* **"**
>
> **Rick Blaine (Humphrey Bogart) to Ilsa Lund (Ingrid Bergman) in** *Casablanca* **(1942)**

Housed in the Palais are several museums, though some are in the process of being transferred on account of a fire which damaged and closed the Musée des Monuments Français, the Musée du Cinéma Henri Langlois and its adjacent screening room known as the Cinemathèque Français. The latter two are being reopened and incorporated into the Museum of the Seventh Art: Film and the Moving Image in the Palais de Tokyo (*see page 26*).

French Monuments Museum

The **Musée des Monuments Français** is not one of the city's better museums, but when it reopens it may have been spruced up a little. Previously it showed the development of public monuments in France, including statues and murals. It was founded in 1880 by Eugène Emmanuel Viollet-le-Duc, who was responsible for the extensive restorations in Notre-Dame in the 19th century.

Museum of the Sea

Also inside the Palais is the **Musée de la Marine** (*open 1000–1800 Wed–Sun*), which contains exactly what you would expect: scale models of ships (some incredibly finely detailed), models of naval battles, mementoes of naval heroes, paintings, figureheads from ships, exhibitions on maritime life and so forth.

Museum of Mankind

Of much more general interest is the **Musée de l'Homme**, which is upstairs (*open 0945–1715 Wed–Mon*). The museum has been subject to some debate recently as to what should be done with it, as it has rather lagged behind the extensive modernisation programme which has seen many of Paris's museums transformed. It has been modernised to a large extent, but not quite in the imaginative way that has seen, for instance, the Galerie de l'Évolution (*see page 64*) turn into a wonderful state-of-the-art museum.

The Musée de l'Homme, nevertheless, is well worth visiting, certainly if you have children with you. There are plenty of computer screens around the place, though at the moment with information and games in French only. The museum has an admirable collection of the artefacts of mankind, including an enjoyable room full of musical instruments from many cultures, with a small stage in one corner where occasional concerts are given. One gallery shows the evolution of mankind with a timeline diorama that helps you make sense of the various prehistoric periods, and there is an excellent collection of American Indian items, including tents, clothing, head-dresses and weapons.

Outside the Palais, the gardens lead down towards the Seine, either side of a large pool and fountain which is impressively floodlit at night – making for a memorable night-time scene as you gaze across the river to the floodlit Eiffel Tower, counting down the days to the end of the 20th century.

The Palais de Tokyo

This graceful building was constructed as the Electricity Pavilion for the World Exhibition held in Paris in 1937. Its west wing is presently being worked on as it will be housing a new Museum of the Seventh Art: Film and the Moving Image, though no opening date has yet been set. Also in here will be the **Musée du Cinéma Henri Langlois,** *which is having to be moved from its previous home in the Palais de Chaillot as a result of fire damage.*

The museum has a collection of some 5000 objects, which tell the story of cinema from its very first days when it developed from still photography. The collection contains cameras, posters, complete film sets (including a street scene from *Les Enfants du Paradis*), models used in films, models of film studios and costumes worn by stars like Rudolph Valentino, Marilyn Monroe and Greta Garbo.

City of Paris Museum of Modern Art

The east wing of the Palais contains the **Musée d'Art Moderne de la Ville de Paris** – a changing collection of work, currently enhanced by items from the Beaubourg's Musée National d'Art Moderne while the Beaubourg is being renovated. The resident collection is shown in large, bright galleries, which allow plenty of space for both the art works and the visitors. Some of the works need space as many of the canvases are huge, including the largest painting in the world. This is *Fée Électricité* by Raoul Dufy, a work commissioned by the electricity board for the World Exhibition, and consisting of over 250 panels and a video display telling the story of the development of electricity since the days of the earliest Greek scientists and thinkers. It is an awesome work of some 600m square which curves round the walls of one gallery in a vivid blending of colours.

There are many more famous names with works in this collection, including the Cubism of Picasso and Braque, dance sequences by Matisse, surreal and abstract works, and pieces by Modigliani, Chagall, Utrillo, Valadon and Kandinsky amongst many others. The museum also has an experimental centre – the ARC (*Animation, Recherche, Confrontation*) – which has temporary exhibitions of challenging new works, incorporating video, music, sculpture and computers amongst other approaches to art.

The Alma Bridge

Outside, small terraces of steps lead down towards the Seine, past statuary which includes work by Antoine Bourdelle (1861–1929), who studied under Rodin – though this part of the Palais is a little neglected and often occupied by skateboarding youngsters. To the east is the **Pont de l'Alma** – a bridge which was originally built in 1855 (and rebuilt in the 1970s) to commemorate a French victory over the Russians in the Crimean War. A statue of a soldier incorporated into the bridge's design and known as the Zouave survived the rebuilding of the bridge and is still used as a watermark when the level of the Seine rises. It is said that during a flood in 1910 the water reached the Zouave's chin. Nowadays *bateaux-mouches* leave from the quay beneath the bridge for their Seine cruises.

> *There are two gestures now considered typically French: kissing as a form of greeting, and frequent handshaking. Both were once typically English, and caused much wonder to French visitors. Kissing was the normal form of English greeting in the reign of Elizabeth I. In the nineteenth century 'le handshake' was imported from England by dandies; there even used to be professors who gave lessons in Paris on how to shake hands.*

Theodore Zeldin, *The French* (Collins, 1983)

Getting there: 11 Avenue de Président Wilson.

Hôtel des Invalides

*The whole area of Les Invalides takes its name from the **Hôtel des Invalides** (* Place des Invalides *), bearing in mind that the use of the French word* hôtel *has a wider definition than its English counterpart, meaning a town-house as well as a hotel for paying guests.*

This vast *hôtel* was built as a home for invalid soldiers on the orders of Louis XIV, embarrassed by the fact that many of his former soldiers who had been invalided out of the army were reduced to begging in the streets. It was finally completed in 1676 and provided shelter for 4000 elderly ex-soldiers. Even today a handful of pensioners still live there: you can see some of their houses if you use the entrance to the east of the golden-domed Église du Dôme.

The Army Museum

The bulk of the building now houses the **Musée de l'Armée** (*open 1000–1700 daily*). It is a huge collection for a huge building, running round the central courtyard of the Hôtel and containing whole armies of armour, including that for children and horses, and from the Orient as well as from France. There are also models of battlefields, paintings, campaign flags, swords, shields, crossbows, rifles, maces and maps. Storage rooms can be seen in which further enormous collections of weaponry are held. Not surprisingly, the armies and artefacts of Napoléon play a great part, including his campaign tent and his bed. More modern warfare is represented by way of two large rooms, each given over to the two world wars, and more recent still are exhibits on the modern world of the Secret Service.

Église du Dôme

Behind the Hôtel is the **Église du Dôme**, which some people dismiss as over-ornate and others regard as a masterpiece of the French Classical style. It is one of those buildings which gives you the impression of being inside a wedding cake, with several grand chapels off a circular crypt in the centre, whose rails you look over to gaze down on the tomb of Napoléon, which is suitably Napoleonic. Steps lead down to the crypt for a closer examination, where it can be seen that Bonaparte's legendary short stature is not evident in this memorial. He is buried inside a series of seven coffins, starting with oak on the outside, then ebony, two of lead, one of mahogany and the inside one of tin plate.

> " *Napoléon wanted to turn Paris into Rome under the Caesars, only with louder music and more marble. And it was done. His architects gave him the Arc de Triomphe and the Madeleine. His nephew Napoléon III wanted to turn Paris into Rome with Versailles piled on top, and it was done. His architects gave him the Paris Opera, an addition to the Louvre, and miles of new boulevards.* "

Tom Wolfe, introduction to
***From Bauhaus to Our House* (1981)**

The Dôme is not merely the resting place of Napoléon, however, as it is also the place where other military leaders are laid to rest, including Napoléon's elder brother Joseph, Marshal Foch, who led the armies on the western front in the later stages of World War I, and Marshal Turenne, who fought in the Thirty Years' War of the late 17th century. That is when, like the Hôtel, the church was built, the dome itself reaching an impressive height of 107m (351ft). Its golden outer covering was added in 1715.

Around Les Invalides

The area around Les Invalides is a prosperous one with some splendid houses, which gradually merges into the more Bohemian quarter of St-Germain to the east. The number-one attraction in the immediate vicinity of the Hôtel, and one of the most popular small museums in Paris, is the **Musée Rodin** *(77 Rue de Varenne, open Tue–Sun 1000–1745, closes 1700 in winter).*

The collection is housed in the Hôtel de Biron, which was built in 1730 and bought in 1753 by the wealthy Maréchal-Duc de Biron, who lavished money on the gardens in particular before meeting his end at the guillotine. By the time the sculptor Auguste Rodin (1840–1917) moved in in 1908, it had been converted to a collection of artists' studios. He lived there for the rest of his life, alongside some illustrious neighbours such as Isadora Duncan and Henri Matisse. Although today Rodin is regarded as one of the greatest sculptors of all time, in those days there were periods when he was unable to pay his rent and many of the statues on display were handed over in lieu of money.

THE EIFFEL TOWER AND LES INVALIDES

Born in Paris in 1840, Rodin came to notice – and to notoriety – in 1877, when his statue *The Age of Bronze* was exhibited at the Paris Salon and outraged many people with its powerful physicality: some accused him of taking plaster casts from live models. The power in his work is undeniable, and some of his greatest creations are on display either in the house or in the attractive gardens. Outside is *The Thinker*, as well as *The Burghers of Calais*, while the best-known work inside the house must be *The Kiss*. No matter how familiar it may seem from reproductions, the original still exerts its sensuous magic.

Shopping in Rue Cler

" *The Louvre was wonderful. I spent three hours sketching one of Michaelangelo's slaves. Afterward I hopped on the Métro to try to catch the Rodin museum's last admittance. My luck, it was pouring rain and only the garden was open. Funny how fitting it is to view Rodin's work in the gray Paris mist, soaking cold, the rain tapping softly on black umbrellas. "*

Gina Granados,
'Dear Patrick'

On the far side of the Hôtel des Invalides from the museum, other senses are satisfied in the shops and the market along **Rue Cler**, where the well-heeled ladies of the area patronise the cheese shops, wine merchants, the cafés, the *charcuterie*, the House of Ham, the florists, the butcher, the baker – but no candle-stick maker. The shops are open six days a week, and some of them also on a Sunday morning, while the market is closed on Monday and busiest on Saturday. Davoli, or the House of Ham, at number 34 does superb salads if you want to take a picnic lunch, rounded off perhaps with a strawberry or apricot tart. More elaborate dishes can be bought at number 40, the Ragut Charcuterie, and bread added to your basket at number 42, Le Fournil de Pierre.

There is also an exceptionally good *chocolatier* not far away at 149 Rue de l'Université, where the shop of **Michel Chaudin** has elegant but fun displays of the chocolate-maker's art, including chocolate so rich you could put on weight merely by looking through the window, and elaborately constructed confections in the shape of the Eiffel Tower.

Eating and drinking

While there is no shortage of good – and expensive – places to eat in the area, there are inevitably lots of poor-quality over-priced cafés and restaurants pulling in the tourist crowds close to the Eiffel Tower, so avoid those. There are also plenty of residential streets where – not typical of Paris – you can walk for a couple of blocks and not see a bar or a shop.

Cafés and Bars

Café du Marché

38 Rue Cler. Tel: 47 05 51 27. ££. If you can't get good food here, surrounded by the market stalls of Rue Cler, then you won't get it anywhere. Almost always busy with shoppers and shopkeepers alike, settling in for a snack, a coffee, a beer, a chat and a great view of the passing show. *0700–2400 Mon–Sat, 0800–1600 Sun, food served lunchtime and evenings only.*

Café le Dôme

41 Avenue de la Bourdonnais. Tel: 45 51 45 41. ££. A good non-touristy café/bar/brasserie, which has a view of the Eiffel Tower from one side, and a simple menu including steaks and sandwiches, though you can just sit and sip a coffee if you like. *0700–0200 daily.*

Le Royal Tour

23 Avenue de la Bourdonnais. Tel: 47 05 04 54. ££. Another safe bet within short walking distance of the Eiffel Tower, this immaculate café also serves meals from noon onwards, with simpler snacks and pastries available too. *0600–2400 daily.*

Café Thoumieux

4 Rue de la Comète. Tel: 45 51 50 40. ££. Fashionable tapas bar not far from the Hôtel des Invalides, where you can snack on squid, hot sausage and other tapas specialities, or have a coffee or a cocktail as the noise builds from chatter to a roar over the course of an evening. *1200–0200 Mon–Fri, 1700–0200 Sat.*

Restaurants

Altitude 95

Eiffel Tower. Tel: 45 55 20 04. ££. This surprisingly good and not-too-expensive bistro is on the 95m (312ft) high first floor of the Eiffel Tower and has impressive views – so book a table near the windows well in advance if you can. With such a location you might expect less attention to the food, but that is not the case. There is a rotating menu which covers various French regions, in a good and imaginative way. *1130–1500 and 1830–2200 daily.*

Au Bon Accueil

14 Rue Monttessuy. Tel: 47 05 46 11. ££. A short walk from the foot of the Eiffel Tower is this, one of the best bistros in the district. Exceptional food, depending on what is best in the market at the time, combined with affordable prices, means that booking is essential. *1200–1430 Mon–Fri and 1930–2215 Mon–Sat, closed Aug.*

Le Violon d'Ingres

135 Rue St-Dominique. Tel: 45 55 15 05. £££. Run by fashionable chef Christian Constant (*see page 12*), this is the place to taste the best of what's happening in contemporary French cuisine. Booking essential. *1200–1430 and 1900–2230 Mon–Fri, closed Aug.*

Shopping

Clubs and nightlife

This is not a district throbbing with nightlife, other than the sounds of people eating. Instead take a short walk to St-Germain and the Left Bank (see page 50).

From souvenir tack around the Eiffel Tower to swish shops as you head east towards the Hôtel des Invalides, this area covers both extremes. For food shopping a visit to **Rue Cler** *is essential (see page 31). The shop at the* **Musée d'Art Moderne de la Ville de Paris** *has an excellent range of books, prints, postcards and other imaginative gift ideas. A typical vast French department store, particularly good for clothes, is* **La Clef des Marques** *at 99 Rue St-Dominique, to the north of Hôtel des Invalides, while along the same street at number 76 is* **Toutes Griffes Dehors***, which sells end-of-line bargains, including some designer labels.*

" *The shortest way out of Manchester is notoriously a bottle of Gordon's gin; out of any businessman's life there is the mirage of Paris; out of Paris, or mediocrity of talent and imagination, there are all the drugs, from subtle, all-conquering opium to cheating, cozening cocaine.* "

William Bolitho, 'Twelve Against the Gods' in *Cagliostro (and Seraphina)* **(1930)**

In the sewers of Paris

*'Under the Bridges of Paris' is the romantic side of the city, while under the streets is the less-romantic face: the city's sewers, **Les Égouts**. The entrance is by a bridge, the Pont de l'Alma, on the south side of the river. Here a ticket office marks the entrance to one of the most unusual and popular tours you can take.*

Steps lead down into a dank underworld, where sections of the sewer network have been turned into a visitor attraction – though they are still part of the working sewer system and access may be restricted if there has been particularly heavy rain. This is one of the many hazards facing workers, as explained in the displays. The sewers can fill rapidly in strong downpours, and one man must always keep watch in order to alert his fellow-workers to the possible danger, as rain literally floods into the system from all over the city and the sewer levels rise like a tidal wave.

Guided tours

There are regular guided tours, led by sewer workers, or you can simply wander round the accessible parts by yourself using the map in the leaflet – aided by the fact that the sewers you see all carry the name of the street which they're beneath.

There need be no worries about wandering off into some subterranean network, as the public part is fenced off, and well-lit and supervised. Nevertheless it is a damp and occasionally smelly insight into what gushes through the pipes of a system that contains some 2100km of tunnels – long enough if laid end-to-end to stretch all the way from Paris to Istanbul.

The refuse of Paris

Other statistics abound, such as that Parisians eat 3 million baguettes and 100 tons of fish a day, all of which, along with everything else they eat and drink, and carelessly discarded rubbish, eventually end up in the sewerage system. Work on a proper sewerage system only began in 1825. Prior to that the main way of disposing of all waste was the Seine, which also just happened to be the main water supply. The tour includes a short film, and there are some unusual souvenirs to be had in the gift shop at the end!

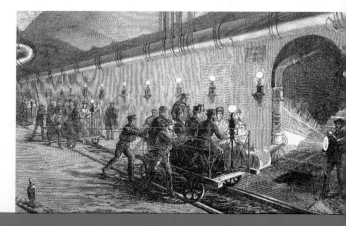

St-Germain

To many visitors – and many residents – the area of St-Germain and its neighbouring Latin Quarter (see pages 54–71) simply are Paris. Everything is here: cafés, bars, nightlife, bookshops, food, drink, galleries, little parks, grand boulevards, the Seine. This is the Paris of Hemingway and Fitzgerald, of Jean-Paul Sartre and Simone de Beauvoir, of the oldest café in the world and some of the most famous, like Les Deux Magots. It also has an unmissable museum in the Musée d'Orsay – an inspired conversion of an old railway station.

ST-GERMAIN

BEST OF
St-Germain

Getting there: **Métro:** *For the Jardin du Luxembourg, Notre-Dame des Champs, St-Sulpice or Odéon; for the Boulevard St-Germain, St-Germain; for upmarket shopping, Rue du Bac or Sèvres-Babylone; for the Musée d'Orsay, Solférino.* **RER:** *The Musée d'Orsay has a station named after it; for the Jardin du Luxembourg, Luxembourg.* **Buses:** *For the Jardin du Luxembourg 21, 27, 38, 82, 84, 85 or 89; for the Musée d'Orsay 24, 63, 68, 69, 73, 83, 84, 94; for St-Germain 39, 48, 63, 70, 86, 87, 95, 96.*

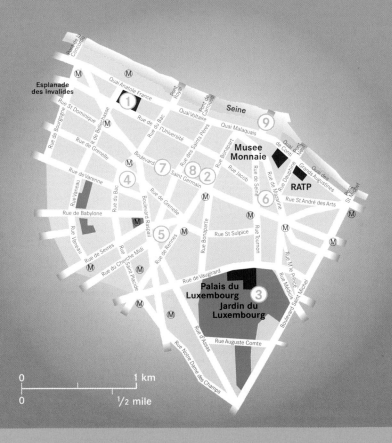

① The Musée d'Orsay

It's hard to choose between the collections at the Louvre and here at the Musée d'Orsay, but while the Louvre can be overwhelming – not to say tiring – this bright new museum, with its compact but high-quality collection, will disappoint no one.
Pages 40–41

② Coffee at Les Deux Magots

Hemingway haunts around the world may be ten a penny, but this café retains a strong feel of what it must have been like when he drank and talked with Scott Fitzgerald and other 'Yanks in Paris' in the 1920s. It still bills itself as the home of artists and intellectuals. **Page 48**

③ Stroll in the Jardin du Luxembourg

This 60-acre park in the built-up and busy St-Germain district has always had a special place in the affections of Parisians. Napoléon dedicated the gardens to children, and they are a pleasant place in which to stroll and relax away from the traffic.
Pages 46–47

④ See the Musée Maillol

Aristide Maillol may not be one of the better-known artists, but his sculptures are distinctive and forceful, and this museum dedicated to his work is well worth seeking out. **Page 42**

⑤ Buy bread from Lionel Poilâne

The number-one baker in France, let alone Paris, has this tiny shop in the district, where you can buy a range of his breads to check out the quality.
Page 43

⑥ Shop in Rue de Buci

The market here has all the noise and hurry that a street market should, with a vast range of foods for sale that will help make up a good picnic lunch or some tasty reminders to take home with you. **Page 43**

⑦ Walk down Boulevard St-Germain late on a Sunday morning

This long street which loops round like a boomerang below the Seine *is* St-Germain, and on a Sunday morning in particular it comes alive with coffee-seekers and church-goers alike, and tourists too come to sit in one or other of its famous cafés. **Pages 42–43**

⑧ Have another coffee, this time at Café de Flore

Close by Aux Deux Magots is its great rival, Café de Flore, with just as many literary and intellectual associations – and just as good for people-watching.
Pages 48 and 53

⑨ See the Pont des Arts

To walk between St-Germain and the Louvre on the Right Bank, take this footbridge, the first iron bridge in Paris, and popular at night with romantic strollers and buskers.

" *It is said that the world's first café opened in Istanbul (the Turks were great popularizers of coffee) in 1550. Paris got its first one in 1686, when a Sicilian named Francesco Procopio dei Coltelli opened an establishment called Le Procope on the Left Bank, on what is now the Rue de l'Ancienne Comédie. It is still in existence on the same site, having closed and opened several times – reviving most recently in 1952 as a restaurant now mainly patronized by tourists, who may or may not be impressed by the fact that Voltaire, Diderot, and Rousseau drank on the premises.* "

Angela Mason, 'Café Society',
Los Angeles Times Magazine

The Musée d'Orsay

*From the outside this museum looks unusual, perhaps
even unlikely, as you do appear to be entering the
glass-arched railway station that it once was. Inside,
however, the station building has been transformed
into a breathtaking and innovative display area.
The museum's wonderful collection, particularly of
Impressionist works, means that it has to be at the
top of the list for anyone's first visit to Paris.*

The museum is incredibly popular, so to avoid too much
queuing you should aim to arrive at least 15 minutes before
opening time. Leave it much later and the queues will be
enormous, and will stay that way for most of the morning.
The advantage of early arrival is that once through the
doors you can have some of the galleries almost to yourself.

Van Gogh

The museum has a strong collection of works by Vincent Van
Gogh (1853–90), some of which you will recognise – like the
Portrait of Doctor Paul Gachet and the painting of the artist's
own room in Arles – and some of which you may not. There
are some strong and mesmerising self-portraits, giving us
glimpses into the painter's tortured soul. Van Gogh only

began painting in 1880,
and was dead by his
own hand ten years later.
From 1886 to 1888 he
lived with his brother
Theo in Paris, where he
became familiar with
the exciting new work of
the Impressionists, and
was inspired by the
countryside of Provence
when he moved there in 1888 for a short but artistically
supercharged period.

The Impressionists

There are too many great artists represented in these galleries to do them all justice here, but highlights include paintings, pastels and sculptures by Edgar Degas – notably his statues and paintings of graceful dancers – and the unflinching look of *The Absinthe Drinker*. Several works by Renoir include tender portraits of bathing nudes and the wonderful handling of light and shade in *Bal du Moulin de la Galette*. Claude Monet is also well represented, as is Manet: his controversial *Le Déjeuner sur l'Herbe* is a huge and arresting canvas. There are also other fine works by Pissarro, Sisley and Cézanne.

Post-Impressionists and Neo-Impressionists

A room devoted to Gauguin includes not only some of his paintings from the South Seas, but sculptures too and even his own design for the front of his house there. The museum has large collections of pastels kept in low-light rooms to avoid damage to the delicate works. One such room is given over to the work of Toulouse-Lautrec, ranging from blunt portraits of prostitutes and dancers to an astonishingly tender scene of two boys asleep in a huge comfy bed. Other artists represented include Rousseau, Bernard, Seurat and Matisse.

Other works

The middle level of the museum is given over to paintings, sculptures and fine-art objects from the late 19th and early 20th centuries, including work by Rodin and Burne-Jones, while the ground level covers the period 1848–70, including photography and the decorative arts as well as paintings and sculptures.

Information

The museum is on the Quai d'Orsay, opposite the Louvre. It is open 0900–1800 Tue–Wed, Fri–Sat (*opens only at 1000 in winter*), 0900–2145 Thur (*opens 1000 in winter*) and 0900–1800 Sun. Closed Mon. Tel: 40 49 48 14 or for recorded information on 45 49 11 11. It has a restaurant and a cafeteria, and a large bookshop.

Boulevard St-Germain

The Boulevard St-Germain begins near the Pont de la Concorde, with the vast open space of the Place de la Concorde visible across the river. The boulevard swings round and runs through St-Germain, more or less parallel to the Seine, before passing through the Latin Quarter and rejoining the river at the Pont de Sully, which leads across to the Île St-Louis. It is a good walk along a great street, with a few entertaining side diversions along the way.

Where the boulevard meets the Métro at Rue du Bac, head south down Boulevard Raspail and look for the shop of Japanese designer **Kenzo** at number 17, at the junction with Rue de Grenelle. Walk west along this street and look on your left for the **Fontaine des Quatres Saisons** (Four Seasons Fountain). This was built in 1739, not merely as decoration (if indeed its elaborate nature is thought decorative) but to provide water to the people who lived in this wealthy part of Paris.

> " *Every city has a sex and an age which have nothing to do with demography. Rome is feminine. So is Odessa. London is a teenager, an urchin, and, in this, hasn't changed since the time of Dickens. Paris, I believe, is a man in his twenties in love with an older woman.* "
>
> **John Berger, *Harper's* (New York, Jan 1987)**

The Musée Maillol

Just beyond the unmissable fountain is the entrance to the **Musée Maillol** (*1100–2000 Wed–Mon*), devoted to the work of sculptor and painter Aristide Maillol (1861–1944). The collection was put together by Dina Vierny, whom the artist met in 1934 when she was 15. He said that she was the inspiration for work he had already done, and she became his model and companion for the last ten years of his life. His paintings and sculptures of her and other women combine tenderness with eroticism. The house also contains changing exhibitions and work that belonged to Maillol, such as by Matisse, Bonnard, Dufy and Kandinsky. An attractive café has been built into the basement, with works of art to gaze at while you eat or have a coffee.

Slightly out of the way, further down the Boulevard Raspail and off to the left, is the bread shop of **Lionel Poilâne** (*8 Rue du Cherche-Midi*). It is considered the finest bread in France, all made in 24 wood-fired ovens by 24 bakers each working his own oven. Poilâne has even made bread sculptures for Salvador Dali, and some of the finest restaurants mention the bread by name if they serve it or use it in recipes.

Churches, cafés and markets

Rejoining Boulevard St-Germain and continuing east, it isn't long before you reach the **Café de Flore** and **Les Deux Magots** (*see page 48 for further information*). Time for a coffee at one or the other to watch the passing parade. Further on, to the left, is the church that gives the street and district its name: **St-Germain-des-Prés** (St Germanus of the Meadows, which were what was here back in Roman times). St Germanus (496–576) was a Bishop of Paris, and the present building dates back to the 12th century.

Just beyond the church, look for the left turn down **Rue de Buci**. There is a market here every day except Monday, busiest on Saturday and Sunday mornings, with some fine-quality foodstuffs for sale, both local and imported, fresh and preserved. Beyond here the Boulevard St-Germain continues on into the Latin Quarter, crossing the Boulevard St-Michel, which more or less marks the border.

43

Boulevard St-Michel

During the reign of Napoléon III (1852–70), a French civil servant and urban planner named Georges-Eugène Haussmann, later to become Baron Haussmann (1809–91), redesigned Paris to create the look of the city which we enjoy so much today. Haussmann created long, wide boulevards and more parks, and moved the old railway stations away from the very city centre. **Boulevard St-Michel** *was one of these new streets, cutting south from the Seine through the Left Bank. It was named in 1867 after the former chapel of St-Michel, which once stood close to its northern end where it reaches the Seine at Pont St-Michel.*

St-Mich', as it's known, runs as straight as a Roman road, and to the east of it is the Latin Quarter, to the west is St-Germain. A walk along its length, diverting into the side streets, covers many different aspects of Paris's history.

Place St-Michel

Start at **Place St-Michel**, where a cluster of cheap restaurants appeal to visitors on a budget and to the local students (the Sorbonne is not far away). In the Place is the Fontaine St-Michel, a 25m-high creation of St Michael fighting a dragon. Rue de la Harpe and Rue de la Huchette, both of which branch off to the east, are amongst the oldest streets in Paris, dating back to medieval times. In those days the latter street was the Street of the Roasters, filled as it was with barbecue pits – not far removed from today's souvlaki grillers and other cheap eateries. At number 10 in 1795 Napoléon Bonaparte once lived, while at the Théâtre de la Huchette the Absurdist playwright Ionesco's play *The Bald Prima-Donna* has been running without a break since 1957.

Shakespeare and Company

Off to the west of the boulevard, down Rue de l'Odéon, number 12 was once the site of the most famous bookstore in Paris, **Shakespeare and Company**, which was here from 1921 until 1940. It was run by Sylvia Beach, an American woman dedicated to literature, and her shop was a second home – and often a loan office – to ex-pat writers such as Ezra Pound, Thornton Wilder, Scott Fitzgerald and, inevitably, Ernest Hemingway. Beach was, however, devoted to one writer in particular, the Irishman James Joyce. She it was who first published his novel *Ulysses* in 1922, which was banned in Britain and for many years only available here in Paris. The shop still exists but is now in Rue de la Bûcherie in the Latin Quarter (*see page 66*).

" *I stood in the place St-Michel, with its obligatory postcard Parisian fountain, suitcase in hand, gaping up the boulevard. It was a good two hours after pub closing time at home but everywhere was streaming with people. It was more like a fairground than a street, the ever-replenishing crowds visiting the terraced cafés as if they were sideshows.* "

Peter Lennon, *Foreign Correspondent* (Picador 1994)

West of Rue de l'Odéon is **Place St-Sulpice**, a pleasant place for a break with its Café de la Mairie (*see page 48*), fountain, trees and a couple of Yves Saint-Laurent stores. The huge church in the square was begun in 1646 and took 134 years to complete. In a side chapel to the right as you enter are some murals by Delacroix. The church once hosted a banquet for 1200 people to celebrate Napoléon's victory in Egypt.

Jardin du Luxembourg (Luxembourg Gardens)

These 60 acres of formal gardens stretch south from the Palais du Luxembourg and are a popular spot for mothers and their children, for strolling couples, boules-players, chess-players, model-boat sailors and anyone wanting to enjoy the occasional free concert or just get away from the noise of the streets into the park's avenues lined with statues. Park and palace were both built by Marie de Médicis (1573–1642), the widow of King Henri IV, who after the king's assassination in 1610 wanted both gardens and palace to remind her of her original home of Florence.

The gardens (*open 0730–2130 daily in summer, 0815–1700 daily Nov–Mar*) have a number of facilities, such as tennis courts, a puppet theatre, a children's playground, pony rides, schoolchildren's tricycle races and a pear orchard, the fruit of which can be bought during the Expo-Automne held here every year in the last week of September. There is even a bee-keeping school and an apiary, whose curator gives classes on bee-keeping throughout the summer. There is a miniature version of the Statue of Liberty, and many statues of French queens and prominent women of the 19th century, as well as a small museum in the grounds which houses temporary exhibitions in the summer. In Hemingway's novel *Islands in the Stream* his poverty-stricken hero catches the Jardin's pigeons in order to have something to eat, while the dancer Isadora Duncan used to come into the gardens at dawn to practise. Such are the quirky delights of the Jardin du Luxembourg. Little wonder, then, that when Baron Haussmann, during his remodelling of Paris (*see page 44*), wanted to transform the gardens, such was the strength of feeling from the Parisians that he abandoned his plans.

Palais du Luxembourg (Luxembourg Palace)

This was to be modelled on Marie de Médicis' family home, the Palazzo Pitti in Florence, and work began in 1615. However, by the time it was completed in 1631 Marie had been banished by her son, Louis XIII. It was at one time a prison and was the headquarters of the German Luftwaffe during the occupation of World War II, but it still houses the French Senate (the Upper House), who have sat here since 1804. It is only open to the public on the first Sunday of each month, and the compulsory guided tour must be booked before the 15th of the previous month (*tel: 44 61 20 89 or 44 61 21 69*). Inside there is a library decorated with paintings by Delacroix, and a Garden Book Room with 17th-century panelling and paintings that were once in Marie de Médicis' private apartments.

Fontaine de Médicis

One of the focal points of the Jardin is this fountain, which was built for Marie in 1624. It stands imposingly at the end of a long pond filled with goldfish, around which is a pleasant place to sit, in the shade of the plane trees.

Eating and drinking

St-Germain is one of the magnets for tourists and Parisians alike, all in search of good food and drink, by day or by night. They may not always end up in the same places, though, as there are some restaurants that try to tempt the tourists in, and others which the locals head for because they know them. Always be suspicious if a restaurant employs someone outside trying to talk you into going inside. There are enough discriminating diners in Paris for that not to be necessary, though it all adds to the buzz of the place.

Cafés and Bars

Les Deux Magots
170 Boulevard St-Germain. Tel: 45 48 55 25. ££. Famous not only for its literary past (see Hemingway's *A Moveable Feast*) but for its summer sidewalk show of buskers. A great place for a coffee, or for something stronger. *0730–0200 daily, closed Aug.*

Café de Flore
172 Boulevard St-Germain. Tel: 45 48 55 26. ££. Where Sartre and de Beauvoir 'more or less set up house', according to the intellectual's memoirs, and before them artists like Dali and Duchamp hung out here. Serves snacks and salads as well as drinks (coffee or stronger), with hot grog its winter speciality. *0700–1400 daily.*

Café de la Mairie
8 Place St-Sulpice. Tel: 43 26 67 82. £. A great place to relax, slightly away from the St-Germain crowds and handy for the Jardin du Luxembourg. Popular young hang-out and people-watching spot. *0700–0200 Mon–Sat, food 1100–0200.*

Au Petit Suisse
16 Rue de Vaugirard. Tel: 43 26 03 81. £. Historic and atmospheric mix of café and tabac in maze-like building. Good wines and other drinks but only sandwiches and snacks to eat. *0700–2000 Mon–Fri, closed Aug.*

Restaurants

L'Épi Dupin

11 Rue Dupin. Tel: 42 22 64 56. ££.
This is one place much sought after by
discriminating Parisians and visitors
who have done their homework – so
much so that for their busy Friday
night you normally have to book at
least three weeks ahead. It's a bright
and bustling smart-casual place,
which bakes its own bread, serves
imaginative dishes and won't break
the bank. *1200–1430 and 1930–2330,
Mon–Fri, closed most of Aug.*

Alcazar

*62 Rue Mazarine. Tel: 53 10 19 99.
£££.* This Brit-owned brasserie in the
heart of St-Germain was a bold venture
by Sir Terence Conran. Stylish décor, as
you would expect, but excellent classic
French food too, like duckling in honey
and spices. Not cheap, but a less-
expensive bar menu is also available.
1200–1500 and 1800–0200 daily.

Aux Fins Gourmets

*213 Boulevard St-Germain. Tel: 42 22
06 57. ££.* Long-established favourite
on the Boulevard, which dishes up fine
traditional fare in its fine traditional
surroundings. Simple meals such as
cassoulet and roast lamb are well
done, and as unfancy as the décor.
*1200–1500 Tue–Sat and 1930–2200
Mon–Sat, closed Aug.*

Le Bamboche

*15 Rue de Babylone. Tel: 45 49 14 40.
££.* A newish bistro that became
quickly popular thanks to its excellent
– if not inexpensive – menu, offering
fresh fish such as cod and turbot, or
lobster, all served with unusual and
imaginative sauces. Booking advisable
for the evenings. *1200–1430 and
2000–2300 Mon–Fri, closed Aug.*

Le Récamier

*4 Rue Récamier. Tel: 45 48 86 58.
£££.* Paris abounds in good regional
restaurants, and this Burgundian place
serves the produce of the region whose
dishes are as hearty as its more robust
wines. You don't have to have the
calves' brains, but much of the menu is
meat-based – even down to the snails
in garlic. Vegetarians look elsewhere,
carnivores look to your credit cards.
1200–1400 and 1900–2230 Mon–Sat.

Gaya Rive Gauche

44 Rue du Bac. Tel: 45 44 73 73. £££.
A treat for fish-lovers, this tiny place
(only five tables plus bar seating, so
book) has a long menu including
monkfish, brill, skate, red mullet, fish
soups, shellfish and salads – in fact,
just about the only non-fishy area is
the pudding menu. *1215–1430 and
1715–2300 Mon–Sat.*

“ … the Closerie des Lilas, a bar-restaurant at the junction of boulevard
St-Michel and boulevard Montparnasse … When I sat waiting at the bar
my elbow touched a plaque marking the spot where Hemingway used to
drink. I moved away in scorn to a corner table. ”

Peter Lennon, *Foreign Correspondent* (Picador, 1994)

Clubs and nightlife

Le Bilboquet

13 Rue St-Benoît. Tel: 45 48 81 84.
Free admission, drinks ££. Smart bar/
restaurant which has live jazz every
evening, including overseas artists.
The music doesn't start till late, so time
to dine first. *2100–dawn, Mon–Sat.*

Caveau de la Huchette

5 Rue de la Huchette. Tel: 43 26 65 05.
£. In the cellar of a building on one of
the oldest streets in Paris is this jazz
club, which covers everything from
swing to be-bop, with a few jazz-rock
bands too. *2130–0200 Mon–Fri,*
2130–0400 Sat–Sun.

La Closerie des Lilas

171 Boulevard Montparnasse. Tel: 43
54 21 68. ££. Classic jazz piano-bar
venue just south of the Jardin du
Luxembourg. *2200–0100 daily.*

Maison des Cultures du Monde

101 Boulevard Raspail. Tel: 45 44 41
42, ££. Small theatre that hosts plays
and concerts from companies all over
the world. Check a current listings
magazine for details.

Les Latitudes Jazz Club

7–11 Rue St-Benoît. Tel: 42 60 23 02.
££. Hotel basement bar with a good
reputation that attracts visiting jazz
stars. *1800–0200 daily, live jazz*
from 2200.

Flash Back

37 Rue Grégoire-de-Tours.
Tel: 43 25 56 70. ££. Techno-rock
disco. *2300–dawn, daily.*

Shopping

Fashion shops, galleries, food shops, cool shops –
St-Germain has them all. Some of the more unusual
stores include:

Barthélémy

51 Rue de Grenelle. Tel: 45 48 56 75.
Specialist cheese shop highlighting
produce from the owner's native
Auvergne, with wine and cheese-
boards too. *0800–1930 Tue–Sat.*

Carton

6 Rue de Buci. Tel: 43 26 04 13. Bakery
and patisserie, with mouth-watering
tartes on display. *0700–2030 Tue–Sun.*

Le Monde en Marche

34 Rue Dauphine. Tel: 43 29 09 49.
Wooden toys, carved puppets and
magic tricks. *1030–1930 Tue–Sat.*

Christian Constant

37 Rue d'Assas. Tel: 45 48 45 51. The
chocoholic's choice, though the shop
does sell other foodstuffs and teas from
around the world. *0800–2000 daily.*

Jean-Paul Hévin

3 Rue Vavin. Tel: 43 54 09 85.
Specialist chocolatier. *1000–1930*
Mon–Sat, 1000–1400 and 1500–1830
Sun, closed Mon in July and Aug.

ST-GERMAIN

Café culture

Cafés in Paris are like cafés should be, and as unlike the archetypal British 'caff' as you can imagine. To begin with they also serve alcohol and usually food too, so whether you want an espresso, a beer, a glass of wine, a sandwich, a salad, a brandy or a cup of tea, you can get them all in the typical Paris café. One thing they

have in common is that your drinks are cheaper if you sit or stand at the bar, more expensive when the waiter serves you at a table.

But cafés are more than just somewhere to sit and have a drink, they are part of the culture of Paris and have always provided retreats for writers, artists, intellectuals and political thinkers. Some have gone there to work, some to talk, some to think about sorting out the world's social problems, some even for a glass of wine and a snack.

Parisians frequent them from dawn till, well, almost round till dawn again, as many cafés open very long hours and, with an estimated 12,000 of them in the city, you're sure to find one that suits you. Few will move you on or make you feel uncomfortable if you want to sit there a while with your paper, nursing a drink.

Writers and philosophers

'Simone de Beauvoir and I more or less set up house in the Flore', Sartre wrote of the Café de Flore on Boulevard St-Germain. 'We worked from 9am till noon, when we went out to lunch. At 2pm we came back and talked with our friends till 4pm, when we got down to work again until 8pm.'

Another writer, the Irish journalist Peter Lennon, observed that 'In Paris bars and cafés, the proximity of a celebrity gave no right of contact, one of the factors which helped [Samuel] Beckett preserve his privacy. When he gave up the Falstaff, eight years and about five hundred steaks *au poivre* later, I still hadn't exchanged a word with Sartre.' That the winner of the Nobel prize for Literature, and two of the world's greatest writers and philosophers, could all sit in cafés unbothered by anyone, is a testimony to the importance that cafés play in the lives of all Parisians, both famous and unknown.

The Latin Quarter

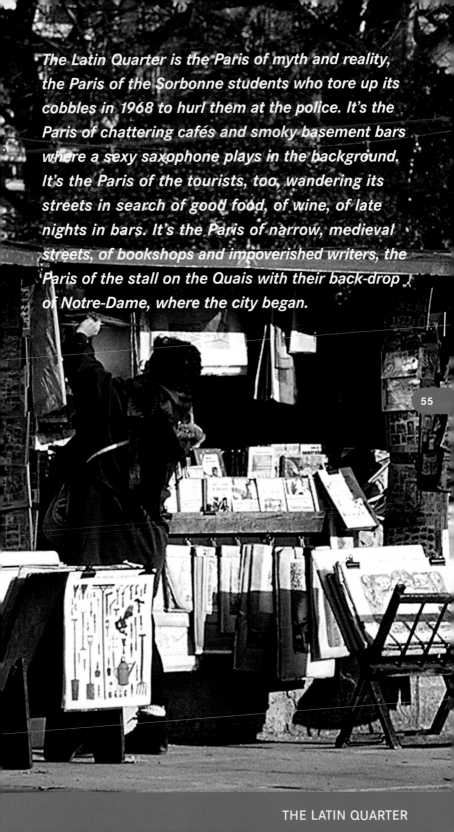

The Latin Quarter is the Paris of myth and reality, the Paris of the Sorbonne students who tore up its cobbles in 1968 to hurl them at the police. It's the Paris of chattering cafés and smoky basement bars where a sexy saxophone plays in the background. It's the Paris of the tourists, too, wandering its streets in search of good food, of wine, of late nights in bars. It's the Paris of narrow, medieval streets, of bookshops and impoverished writers, the Paris of the stall on the Quais with their back-drop of Notre-Dame, where the city began.

BEST OF

The Latin Quarter

Getting there: **Métro:** *St-Michel for the Quais, Maubert-Mutualité to be in the heart of the area, Cluny la Sorbonne for the Sorbonne, and Place Monge for Rue Mouffetard and the Galerie de l'Évolution.* **RER:** *Luxembourg for the Sorbonne and Panthéon, St-Michel–Notre-Dame for the Quais and the heart of the Quarter.* **Bus:** *For the Panthéon 21, 27, 38, 82, 84, 85, 89; for Rue Mouffetard 47; for the Galerie de l'Évolution 24, 57, 61, 63, 65, 89, 91; for the Quais 21, 24, 27, 38, 58, 70, 85, 96.*

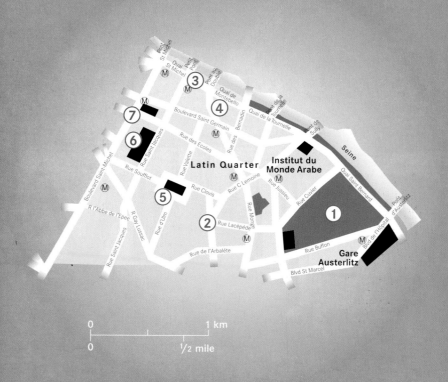

① See the Galerie de l'Évolution in the Jardin des Plantes

This impressive new wing of the Natural History Museum is like an anthropological version of the Musée d'Orsay – a stunningly original display area that kids will love. **Pages 64–65**

② Rue Mouffetard market

Another of Paris's very old streets, it is never busier and better than on weekend mornings, when crowds jam the narrow gaps between the stalls and the colourful shopfront displays. You can put together a picnic for the nearby Jardin des Plantes. **Pages 60–61**

③ See the stalls on the Quais by the Seine

The rows of little stalls that line the Left Bank of the Seine have been here for centuries, selling books, postcards, prints and even a few ordinary souvenirs. Take a Sunday morning stroll, and you might find an unusual and very French gift to take back. **Pages 66–67**

④ Browse for books at Shakespeare and Company

More browsing is to be had at what is probably Paris's best-known bookshop – no longer at its original location but still a jumble of a place with great character and an essential visit for the bookworm. **Pages 66–67**

⑤ Visit the crypts of the Panthéon

Grandiose it may be, but the scale of this temple where the great and the good of Paris are buried is impressive. Don't miss the underground crypts. **Pages 62–63**

⑥ Soak up the Sorbonne atmosphere

Remember *les événements* of 1968 and see whether you think today's students are capable of such protests, as you walk around the streets where it all happened. **Pages 58–59**

⑦ See the stained glass in the Musée de Cluny

You'll never get a better view of some wonderful stained glass than here in this museum in a mansion. **Page 59**

> " *In those days there was no money to buy books. I borrowed books from the rental library of Shakespeare and Company, which was the library and bookstore of Sylvia Beach at 12 rue de l'Odéon. On a cold windswept street, this was a warm, cheerful place with a big stove in winter, tables and shelves of books, new books in the window, and photographs on the wall of famous writers both dead and living.* "

Ernest Hemingway,
A Moveable Feast (1936)

The Sorbonne and the Left Bank

The Sorbonne University (47 Rue des Écoles, courtyard and buildings open to public 0900–1630 Mon–Fri, tel: 40 46 22 11, free) *dates back to 1253, when Robert de Sorbon (a Parisian canon who came originally from the village of Sorbon in the Ardennes) founded a college of theology for 16 poor students. The Sorbonne established itself as the centre for theological study in France and became, and remains, the seat of the University of Paris.*

It was also here that the first printing houses in France were established in 1469, when Louis XI brought three printers from Mainz, thus confirming the site as a centre for learning. Many of the older buildings were restored by Cardinal Richelieu in the early 17th century, when he was Chancellor of the University, and they were rebuilt and extended in the years 1885–1901, confirming the Sorbonne as the most important university in France. It had been closed down during the Revolution, but afterwards Napoléon reopened and revitalised it.

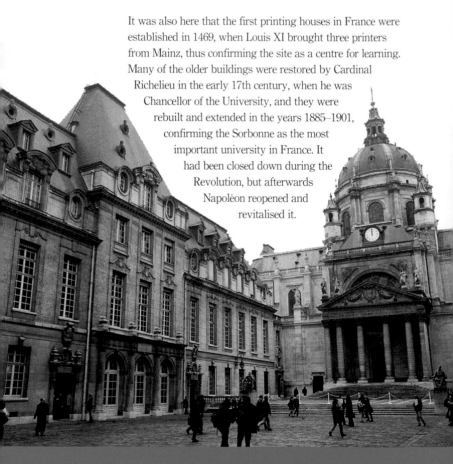

THE LATIN QUARTER

Past students of the Sorbonne have included philosopher Henri Bergson, Egyptologist Jean-François Champollion (who was the first to crack the code of the hieroglyphics), poet Paul Valéry and the physicist André-Marie Ampère.

Église de la Sorbonne

The church overlooking the main courtyard is the **Église de la Sorbonne**, which was built between 1635 and 1642, the year that Cardinal Richelieu died. His white marble tomb is to be found in the chancel, though the chapel is closed to the public except for occasional special exhibitions. If you do get inside you will see hanging above Richelieu's tomb a red hat, reputed to be his, which it is said will fall to the ground when Richelieu's soul is released from Purgatory.

Musée National du Moyen-Âge

Not far from the Sorbonne's main entrance is the **Musée National du Moyen-Âge** (*National Museum of the Middle Ages, 6 Place Paul-Painlevé. Tel: 53 73 78 00. 0915–1745 Wed–Mon*). Formerly known as the **Musée de Cluny**, this collection is housed in the Hôtel de Cluny, one of the oldest private residences in Paris, first built by the abbots of Cluny in 1330 and rebuilt in 1510. It now contains an extensive collection of medieval items, especially tapestries and stained glass. Among the many fine tapestries, the star attraction is the series known as *The Lady and the Unicorn*, thought to have been made in Brussels in the late 15th century although their maker remains unknown. The six separate scenes depict the five senses with a final one showing the lady's mastery of all the senses.

Next to the museum can be seen the remains of Les Thermes (Roman Baths, not open to the public). These are thought to date from about 200 AD, and despite their destruction a century later by the barbarians and subsequent decay over the centuries, the roof of the *frigidarium* (cold bath) has survived.

> " The enduring legend of the Left Bank comes out of the 5th, 6th, 7th and 14th arrondissements: the Latin Quarter, the Sorbonne, the warren of medieval streets near the Place St-André des Arts (including the narrowest street in Paris, the Street of the Fishing Cat – rue du Chat-qui-Pêche), the spirits of Sartre and Genet and Camus at St-Germain-des-Prés, and the ghosts of the painters and writers of Montparnasse, where Gertrude Stein made so many remarks and Hemingway paid attention. "
>
> **Herbert Gold,**
> **'On the Left Bank'**

Rue Mouffetard

Running down from the Sorbonne area on the fringe of the Latin Quarter is one of the loveliest and liveliest streets in Paris, Rue Mouffetard. The area around here has long been a cheap and popular haunt for students, and there are plenty of clothes shops (both cheap and fashionable), busy bars and cafés with great character – and great characters. It has become smarter and more upmarket in recent years, but without losing that Bohemian feel.

The present street dates back to the late 13th century, but the origins of its name are less certain. Some say it means, bluntly, 'Stinking Street' (the French word for a skunk is *mouffette*), or it may have derived from the name of the hill it runs down from: Mont Cétar. There has been a street here since at least Roman times, as in those days it was the main road out of Paris towards the southeast and the Roman town at Lyon, and beyond towards Rome itself. The 'stinking' association comes from the fact that this was for a long time a great area for weaving and tanning, and the animal by-products were dumped into the Bièvre River which ran through here, creating a foul-smelling stream.

Festive market atmosphere

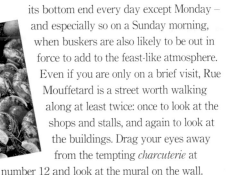

There are no such foul smells today, just tempting ones from the many food shops and stalls that pack the narrow street at its bottom end every day except Monday – and especially so on a Sunday morning, when buskers are also likely to be out in force to add to the feast-like atmosphere. Even if you are only on a brief visit, Rue Mouffetard is a street worth walking along at least twice: once to look at the shops and stalls, and again to look at the buildings. Drag your eyes away from the tempting *charcuterie* at number 12 and look at the mural on the wall. Behind the wall at number 60 is one of the fountains which Marie de Médicis had built in 1624 to take the overflow from the Arcueil Aqueduct, which carried water to her newly-built Luxembourg Palace (*page 47*).

At number 64 is a fascinating old shoe shop, whose owner still makes rubber boots and the wooden shoes known as *sabots* for the more robust of the local traders such as fishmongers and butchers. The shop dates back over 100 years. At number 122 look for the sign showing two boys taking water from a spring, which dates back to about the end of the 16th century and is the oldest street sign on the endlessly interesting Rue Mouffetard. At number 141 is the Église St-Médard, which dates back to the middle of the 15th century, when it was the parish church for the small market town which then existed here, to the south of what was then Paris.

Finally, and far from least, Rue Mouffetard means food shops. Here are cheese shops and *charcuteries*, butchers, bakers and fishmongers, grocers and fruit stalls – a true assault on the senses and a sign of how times have changed for 'Stinking Street'.

> *The crowds thickened, the stalls multiplied, the smells solidified, and one was swept along the sweating, food-smeared cobbles into a gleaming Eldorado of fruit and fish and fowl and meat and veg and pasta and pastries and cheeses and wines and herbs and all those 1,001 other comestibles known only to the French.*

Barry Pilton, *An Innocent Abroad: The Paris Years* (Corgi, 1997)

The Panthéon

In 1744 on this, the highest point on the Left Bank, was a semi-ruined church. Louis XV, who was seriously ill at the time, vowed that if he recovered he would replace the church with something more suited to its location. He did recover and the result was the Panthéon, an overwhelmingly grand church whose crypt contains the tombs of many great French people, including Voltaire, Victor Hugo and Marie Curie.

Indeed, so grand is the building that when it eventually began in 1758, funds quickly ran out, not helped by the fact that there were major subsidence problems. The church wasn't completed until 1789, by which time Louis XV had been dead for fifteen years, and the church's architect, Jacques Germain Soufflot, had himself been dead for nine years, the work having been completed by one of Soufflot's pupils named Rondolet. The scale of the project and its design had both been ridiculed, as the church combined a basic Greek cross design with a combination of both Roman and Gothic styles. The result was 110m long, 84m wide and 83m high (361ft x 276ft x 272ft).

The vast Panthéon had only been a church for two years when it was decided that it should instead be a temple to the great men who had died during the period of the Revolution. This was later extended to include later 'greats', and the first woman to be buried here was Marie Curie, who died in 1934. The tombs are in a series of crypts, which run the full length of the building and are accessible down stairs at the far end of the Panthéon from the entrance. The names of the people in each side crypt are carved outside them. An overall plan is also given, if you wish to pay your respects to particular people. Here you will find Voltaire and Rousseau, Émile Zola and Victor Hugo, Louis Braille (with an appropriate plaque in Braille) and Marie Curie.

> " I am haunted, as so many of us are, by the suspicion that Paris knows something other cities don't, that it has an advantage over them somehow, and is handling our brutal century more intelligently. "
>
> **Jan Morris, 'Within the Périphérique'**

Foucault's Pendulum

Up above, the centre of the building is covered by a huge dome supported by an iron framework. It was from this dome that the French physicist, Jean-Bernard-Léon Foucault (1819–68), suspended a 28kg (62lb) brass pendulum to prove publicly what he had already proved privately in 1849: that the earth rotates about its axis. This is indicated by the fact that the freely-swinging pendulum slowly moves around a set of markers on the floor. As the pendulum does not move, it must be the floor which is moving relative to it. The original pendulum is now in the Musée National des Techniques (Science Museum) but a replica still swings slowly and eerily silently across the immense centre of the church (*1000–1745 Apr–Sept, 1000–1200 and 1400–1645 Oct–Mar, Wed–Mon*).

Église St-Étienne-du-Mont

This church standing just behind the Panthéon was consecrated in 1626, although services had been held on this spot for several centuries. One notable feature is the rood screen – the only one which survives in Paris. Some of the stained glass is original, and Pascal and Racine are buried here.

Jardin des Plantes (Botanical Gardens)

These pleasant gardens (0730–1945 summer, 0800–dusk winter, daily, free *) with their museums, menagerie and other features were originally a rubbish heap. Then in 1626 Louis XIII gave his physicians permission to move the Royal Medicinal Herb Garden here from its previous location on the Île de la Cité. The gardens expanded, the Herb Garden evolved into a school for the study of natural history generally as well as pharmacy and botany, and the gardens were formally opened to the public in 1640.*

Natural History Museum

The study of the natural world continues here and the gardens are now the site of the **Musée National d'Histoire Naturelle**. This is spread over several buildings, and most of the collections are really of interest to specialists only: there are galleries devoted to minerology, paleontology, entomology and paleobotany. The star building, however, is the **Galerie de l'Évolution** (*1000–1800 Fri–Wed, 1000–2200 Thur*). This has transformed the traditional image of a natural history museum – cabinets of stuffed animals and rows of birds' eggs – with breathtaking imagination and the help of a theatrical designer, René Allio.

The original cast-iron and glass building was erected in 1889, at

the same time as the Eiffel Tower was being built. It housed the collections that botanists and naturalists had brought back from their travels in the 18th and 19th centuries. It slowly deteriorated, was damaged by bombing in World War II, closed in 1965 and lay abandoned for 20 years. When it reopened it had become a stunning display area, using the original high central space, with galleries around the sides, glass lifts, low lighting, and the idea that it should do more than just display items, it should tell the story of evolution. There are lots of interactive displays, computers with touch-screens, video rooms, a Gallery of Extinct Species – down the central area on the ground floor marches a caravan of animals from the African savannah. Although some of the original collections are used, many new exhibits have been created by making models of the creatures rather than displaying stuffed animals. The vast size of such things as sea elephants can be appreciated up close, and you can gaze straight into the jaws of a shark.

World population count

As you work your way round and up to the higher floors, you come forward in time and learn about the latest developments in DNA. Then you see an illuminated counter which gives the population of the world, and the phenomenal rate at which it is increasing, with hundreds of people being born, and far fewer dying, as you stand and examine it.

" I ate and read with languorous pleasure, recalling musical moments that resonated with Marcus's. Seconds after I came across a reference to 'Bette Davis Eyes' by Kim Carnes, the song began to play on the wine bar's radio. The rain stopped, a bit of sun broke through the grey day and I wished the moment could last forever, so complete did life seem there in that tiny dark café. "

Michele Anna Jordan, 'Paris Rapture'

Outside there are various botanical gardens, a Winter Garden Glasshouse of tropical plants, a Mexican Garden of cacti, the oldest tree in Paris (a false acacia planted in 1635) and an old-fashioned zoo, within which is a Micro Zoo where microscopes and headphones reveal the natural world normally unseen and unheard.

Bookshops

*The Latin Quarter has the most famous bookshop in Paris, **Shakespeare and Company**, but many more besides, with others in the neighbouring St-Germain district and vendors of books, magazines, postcards and prints lining the Quais by the Seine, most particularly on weekend mornings. The whole area is a bookworm and bibliophile's delight.*

The original Shakespeare and Company was in Rue de l'Odéon (*page 45*) and run by Sylvia Beach. When that closed, part of her stock – together with the use of the name – was acquired by George Bates Whitman, a distant relative of the poet Walt Whitman, who still reigns over the present shop, which opened in 1956 at 37 Rue de la Bûcherie. Whitman has continued Beach's support for literary and intellectual Paris, and his shop has been visited by the likes of Henry Miller, J P Donleavy and Lawrence Durrell, but the humble browser looking for an English-language book in among the jumble of shelves and rooms will still get the same warm welcome. The noticeboard outside reveals that the Paris literary scene is alive and well – and in many cases as impoverished as it ever was.

Specialist bookshops

There are many specialist bookshops in this area, though, such as the **Librairie Gourmande** (*4 Rue Dante, tel: 43 54 37 27*), a small shop with a large stock of books ancient and modern, all dealing with the subject of food and wine. It isn't all expensive rare editions, as you can also pick up bargain books on, for instance, French regional cooking that have been remaindered. Next door at number 6 is the rather different **Album** (*tel: 43 54 67 09*), which specialises in the zap-pow world of American vintage comic books. Further down the street at number 9 is **À l'Imagerie** (*tel: 43 25 18 66*), which deals in old prints and posters, with many of the Art Deco and turn-of-the-century posters that look so typically Parisian. A world away from this – and a short walk to 170 Boulevard St-Germain – is **La Hune** (*tel: 45 48 35 85*), which deals with art books and the latest in French literature, and has late-night openings and evening readings. At 14 Rue St-Sulpice is **La Chambre Claire** (*tel: 46 34 04 31*), a photography bookshop with a wide selection, and a gallery of changing exhibitions downstairs.

> " *Shakespeare and Company ... symbolizes part of the special spirit of the city. That spirit extends to the chalkboard notices scrawled outside the door, too, source of some of Paris' prime wisdom and deals, where I found the following: 'Paris bookseller looking for outdoor girl to build cabin in north woods. If she will cook him trout for breakfast every morning, he will tell her dog stories every night.* "
>
> **Donald W George, 'The Liberation of Paris',** *San Francisco Examiner*

Riverside book stalls

For the not-so-latest titles, book browsers make their way along the stalls that line **Quai de Montebello** and **Quai de la Tournelle**, whose *bouquinistes* have been based here for centuries – and sometimes it looks like some of their stock hasn't changed much in that time. Although second-hand books predominate – and obviously mostly French ones – some dealers specialise in such subjects as the cinema, or old magazines. Others sell prints and postcards – even a few erotic old cards peep out here and there.

Eating and drinking

If you can't go to the Latin Quarter and have a good night out, whether your budget is high or low and no matter what your taste in food, then you'll never do it anywhere. There are all kinds of cuisines, aside from some of the best French restaurants, and all kinds of price ranges to cater for everyone from poor students to middling tourists to the Parisian rich. For somewhere special you need to book ahead, but just as much fun can be had from wandering around among the many options.

Cafés and Bars

Café de la Poste
7 Rue de l'Épée-de-Bois. Tel: 43 37 05 58. £. An inexpensive and very pleasant café/bar just off the Rue Mouffetard. Simple dishes like *andouillettes*, or a place to linger over coffee or a glass of wine. *0800–2200 Mon–Fri, food 1200–1430 and 1930–2100, closed most of Aug.*

Café de la Nouvelle Mairie
19–21 Rue des Fossés St-Jacques. Tel: 44 07 04 41. £. Handy for the Panthéon, this smart place mixes chic and students alike, with hot and cold meals and, its speciality, a long list of wines by the glass. *0900–2000 Mon/Wed/Fri, 0900–2400 Tue/Thur, food 1200–1400 except Tue/Thur 1200–2200.*

Le Mouffetard
116 Rue Mouffetard. Tel: 43 31 42 50. £. Busy café that reflects the market atmosphere in Rue Mouffetard, with cheap and hearty *plats du jour*, and don't leave without trying one of their croissants or other bread, all baked on the premises. *0715–2200 Tue–Sat, 0715–2000 Sun, food all day, closed July.*

Le Piano Vache
8 Rue Laplace. Tel: 46 33 75 03. £. Lively student hang-out with live music or DJ most nights – cheap, loud, great for a late night. *1200–0200 Mon–Fri, 2100–0200 Sat–Sun, food 1200–1400.*

Restaurants

Le Reminet
3 Rue des Grands-Degrés. Tel: 44 97 04 24. ££. This small old-fashioned place has a wide *à la carte* menu, plus daily specials written on the blackboard, and also a fixed-price menu. Good vegetarian and fish options but plenty of hearty French meat dishes too. Watch the kitchen get more frantic as the evening wears on. *1945–2215 Tue–Sun and 1200–1400 Wed–Sun.*

Les Bouchons de François Clerc

12 Rue de l'Hôtel Colbert. Tel: 43 54 15 34. ££. This traditional old place with its wooden beams stays out of the £££ bracket – and stays full – by cutting out heavy wine mark-ups. The food is excellent, with a fixed-price four-course meal, and booking is definitely advised. *1200–1400 Mon–Fri, 1930–2230 Mon–Sat.*

Chez Henri au Moulin à Vent

20 Rue des Fossés St-Bernard. Tel: 43 54 99 37. £££. Archetypal Parisian bistro, relaxed atmosphere, not cheap but where you'll find fine examples of dishes such as frogs' legs, lamb, steaks, fish. *1230–1345 and 1930–2215 Tue–Sat, closed Aug.*

Les Fontaines

9 Rue Soufflot. Tel: 43 26 42 80. ££. Rather flash looks belie the quality of the food and the lovely views from the terrace room of this busy bistro. Generous portions of all the typical French dishes, such as leg of lamb or venison, and more innovative ones, such as quail with grapes in a rum sauce – but the rather expensive wine bumps up the price. *1200–1500 and 1930–2300 Mon–Sat.*

L'Huître et Demie

80 Rue Mouffetard. Tel: 43 37 98 21. £/££. A good choice for seafood lovers in this area that's thick with restaurants: lobster, *langoustines*, *bouillabaisse*. You can spend a lot in the evenings, or stick to one of the fixed-price menus: lunchtime's is a great bargain. *1200–1430 and 1900–2330 daily.*

❝ *...the world's most interesting city...* **❞**
Anita Brookner, *Observer*

Clubs and nightlife

Le Paradis Latin

28 Rue du Cardinal-Lemoine. Tel: 43 25 28 28. One of the best floor shows in town, but less well known than the likes of the Lido and the Crazy Horse. Similar format: music, girls, spectacle. *Dinner 2000, show 2145, Thur–Tue.*

Les Trois Maillets

56 Rue Galland. Tel: 43 54 00 79. A jazz club that has branched out and plays all kinds of music, both live and recorded, and has a great piano bar. Based in a 13th-century inn. Repertoire varies enormously, so check up-to-date listings. *1800–0600 daily (or rather nightly).*

Shopping

Rue Mouffetard

See pages 60–61 for details of the market and other shopping here.

See pages 60–61 for details of the market and other shopping here.

Place Monge

Smaller than the market at Rue Mouffetard, this one is nevertheless worth a visit for the good-quality foodstuffs for sale. *Open Wed/Fri/Sun am only.*

Maison Kayser

8 Rue Monge. Tel: 44 07 01 42. Bread shop in the heart of the quarter, with the bakery behind and visible from the shop. Good choice from the tasty *pain au chocolat* to worthier organic options. *0700–2000 Mon/Wed/Fri only.*

Jadis et Gourmande

88 Boulevard du Port-Royal. Tel: 43 26 17 75. Chocolate shop that specialises in novelty items, like Paris landmarks, but also makes a good range of regular chocolates too. *1300–1900 Mon, 0930–1900 Tue–Wed, 0930–1930 Thur–Sat.*

69

jazz joints

Jazz and Paris go hand in hand, and have done so since soon after its arrival at the turn of the century. Black American jazz musicians soon found they were treated better in Paris than at home, both personally and with due respect for their music. The jazz joints of Paris,

THE LATIN QUARTER

and in particular the Left Bank, have thumped down the years to the sounds of Benny Carter, Sidney Bechet, Charlie Parker, Miles Davis and Dizzy Gillespie. It was in Paris where early be-bop musicians began wearing their trademark berets, which they then took home to the States.

All-time greats of the jazz world

The musical influence went both ways, though, as the 1930s style known as the Hot Club of France developed in Paris, its best-known practitioners being the Paris-born jazz violinist Stephane Grappelli and his musical partner, the gypsy jazz-guitarist Django Reinhardt. The quintet they formed, the Quintette du Hot Club de France, played with some of the all-time greats, like George Gershwin and Louis Armstrong. Throughout the 1940s and 1950s there was no doubt that Paris was the jazz capital of the world, and during World War II Django Reinhardt was *the* name in Paris jazz circles. Jazz fans will also remember the great film *Round Midnight*, directed by French film-maker Bertrand Tavernier, which is set in the jazz world of 1950s Paris and captures the feel of the place and the music so well. Herbie Hancock won an Academy Award for the score.

Jazz clubs and festivals

After a period when jazz was eclipsed for a while by the arrival of the rock scene of the 60s and 70s, Paris's jazz scene has re-emerged and continues to be strong and exert its influence. Jazz-rock guitarist John McLaughlin lives in the city, as do many musicians from Africa, fusing jazz and rock with their Afro roots. The city has several jazz festivals such as the Villette Jazz Festival and the Boulogne-Billancourt Jazz Festival, so check a listings magazine like *Pariscope* for current events and up-to-date listings of clubs, or get *Lylo*, the monthly guide to concerts.

The
Islands

The two islands in the Seine are the heart of Paris, where the very first settlers made their homes. They even contain the spot where all distances from Paris are measured: Point Zéro. The larger Île de la Cité is far from quiet – what with the law courts, Notre-Dame and the lesser-known but unmissable Sainte-Chapelle (Holy Chapel) – but the smaller Île St-Louis to the east has a few quiet side streets alongside lively restaurants, great galleries and fashionable shops.

The Islands

*Getting there: **Métro:** Île de la Cité has its own Métro stop of the same name, right in the centre, while the Métro stops at Pont Marie and Sully-Morland are equally convenient for the Île St-Louis. **RER:** There are no RER stations close by the islands. **Buses:** 21, 38, 47, 85, 96 for Île de la Cité, and 24, 63, 67, 86, 87 and 89 for Île St-Louis.*

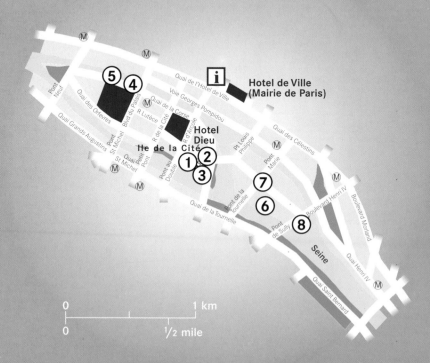

① Join the gargoyles – at the top of Notre-Dame

If people only see one thing on the two islands, then it will naturally and rightly be the medieval masterpiece of Notre-Dame – but to make the most of a visit, climb to the top for views of the city and your chance to do your Charles Laughton impression of the Hunchback of Notre-Dame. **Pages 76–77**

② Go below Notre-Dame, to the Archaeological Crypt

Never mind going 'Under the Bridges of Paris', go under the streets outside Notre-Dame for this great little below-stairs museum which shows you the origins of the city, and how it's looked at different stages of its development. **Pages 76–77**

③ Stand at Point Zéro

Outside Notre-Dame, spare a moment to find Point Zéro, a brass compass that is set into the ground and from which all distances from Paris are measured. **Pages 76–77**

④ See the breathtaking Sainte-Chapelle (Holy Chapel)

This wonderful chapel with its astonishing collection of stained glass is second only to Notre-Dame itself as one of Paris's medieval monuments. As you climb the stairs to the first-floor chapel, nothing prepares you for the sight you will see. **Pages 78–79**

⑤ Visit the Conciergerie, where Marie-Antoinette was imprisoned

In the complex containing the law courts, and opposite the police headquarters of Maigret fame, is the prison used during the French Revolution, where Marie-Antoinette was held for trial. **Page 78**

⑥ Walk around the charming little Île St-Louis

Although the island is too small for you to ever escape the crowds completely, there are some less-busy back-streets and it makes a great place for a haphazard stroll, with some surprising quality shops and eating places. **Pages 80–81**

⑦ Have the best ice-cream in Paris

Berthillon is a long-established favourite among Parisians, where you can buy the best ice-creams and sorbets in the city – but be prepared to queue on a sunny summer day. **Page 82**

⑧ Take a close look at the bridges of Paris

The bridges of Paris are not just famous in song, they've got a fascinating history, and many of them naturally link the islands in the Seine with the Left and Right banks of the river. **Pages 84–85**

Notre-Dame

*La Cathédrale de Notre-Dame de Paris, the Cathedral of Our Lady of Paris, or just plain **Notre-Dame** as everyone knows it, is a masterpiece of medieval architecture, standing solidly alongside the banks of the Seine as it has done for 600 years. Though associated in many people's minds with the Victor Hugo novel from 1831 and subsequent films,* The Hunchback of Notre-Dame *(in 1923 starring Lon Chaney and more memorably in 1939 with Charles Laughton), it has in fact witnessed many great historical events – among them the re-trial of Joan of Arc, the coronation of Henry VI of England and the coronation of Mary Stuart as Queen of France.*

Below ground

This spot by the Seine has been a religious site from almost as soon as Paris was settled. It was first a Gallo-Roman Temple before becoming a Christian basilica, and to see the oldest remains in the cathedral's foundations, visit the fascinating **Crypte Archéologique** (Archaeological Crypt), whose entrance is down some steps in the Place du Parvis Notre-Dame in front of the cathedral (*1000–1730 Apr–Sept, 1000–1630 Oct–Mar, daily*). The dimly-lit museum has been built around the remains, some of which can be illuminated to illustrate certain features, while other displays show the development of some of the other buildings and streets around.

An 800-year history

The foundation stone of Notre-Dame was laid by Pope Alexander III in 1163, during the reign of Louis VII. Despite

a massive workforce who laboured hard, the building was not completed until 1345, after almost 200 years of toil – an indication of the size and scale of the place. Sadly, during the Revolution its rows of statues were decapitated, all but one of the bells were melted down for scrap, and it later fell into disrepair, being used as a storage space for food. It was in fact partly as a result of Victor Hugo's 1831 novel that an order was made in 1841 for the cathedral to be restored – a programme that took a mere 23 years by comparison to its original construction period. The restoration was magnificent, and in recent years it has been thoroughly cleaned to take it back to its original bright splendour.

Inside is the largest organ in France, used for recitals on a Sunday afternoon. Some of the stained glass is glorious: note the building's three famous rose windows, in the north, south and west walls. The fine window in the north wall retains its original 13th-century glass: to see it at its best, visit in the morning. There are many other wonderful windows, and chapels, statuary, wooden carvings and a treasury to see.

Up on the roof

To get to the top of Notre-Dame, climb the 255 steps to the top of the North Tower (signposted via a separate entrance outside), which gives good views not only over the city but of the famous gargoyles. A further 125 steps take you to the top of the South Tower, which contains the 13-ton Emmanuel Bell and has even more splendid views – but don't underestimate the length of the climb. *Cathedral and towers open daily 0900–1930 but closed Saturday 1230–1400.*

66 *An island prime, an island at the secret heart of Paris, floating in time and space across a footbridge on the shady side of the Cathedral of Notre-Dame de Paris, the Île St-Louis may also be the most ambiguous orphan island there is – city and not a city, village and metropolis, provincial and centrally urban, serene and hyped by hundreds of years of noisy lovers of solitude.* 99

Herbert Gold, 'On Île St-Louis'

Sainte-Chapelle and the Île de la Cité

*At the western tip of the Île de la Cité is the **Square du Vert-Galant**, the first part of the name being in English and the second part a reference to the nickname of Henri IV, whose statue stands by the steps leading down to the Square. It translates literally as 'the green gallant', but more accurately means a lusty fellow.*

From Henri's statue, going through the secluded Place Dauphine leads to the Palais de Justice, which contains many government offices and courts and has two main features of interest to visitors. Walk around to the left and look on your right for the entrance to the **Conciergerie** (*0930–1800 Apr–Sept, 1000–1600 Oct–Mar, daily*).

Your first view is of the vast underground Salle des Gens d'Armes (Hall of the Men at Arms), an enormous 1800m square four-aisled 14th-century Gothic hall, still used today for occasional concerts. The main curiosity for most people, though, is the fact that this is the site of the oldest prison in Paris, heavily used during the French Revolution. About 2600 prisoners were held here and condemned to death at the guillotine, the most notable among them being Marie-Antoinette. Her cell and others have been restored to their original state, to give an impression of conditions at the time – worse for some than for the Queen – and in one room a video tells the story of the prison, while those who died are all listed around the walls.

Around the corner from the Conciergerie, and signposted in a courtyard, is the unique twin-chapelled **Sainte-Chapelle** (*0930–1830 Apr–Sept, 1000–1700 Oct–Mar, daily*). It pays to try to get here as early as possible, as the chapel is on many people's itineraries, and its genuinely breath-taking glorious yet intimate nature is best appreciated when there are few other visitors. The double-decker chapel was built by Louis IX in 1248 to house the religious relics he had collected, including most notably the alleged Crown of Thorns and a fragment of the True Cross.

Heaven's door

> " *And the stained glass! Narrow ribs of soaring stone separate band after band of illumination – what seems like more glass than all of Notre Dame in a space one-tenth the size. Colors so exquisite that they seem more real than those we ordinarily know. Shafts of brilliance from every side, as if we'd found our way to the heart of a jewel, to the heart of a dragon's hoard of jewels.* "
>
> **Tim O'Reilly, *'Illumined in Sainte-Chapelle'***

The lower chapel, through which you enter, was reserved for royal servants and other commoners, with the King and Royal Family praying in the chapel above, which is reached up narrow stairways at the rear. When you step out into the upper chapel you are stepping into one of the most-revered buildings in western architecture, once referred to as the Gateway to Heaven. It is only a tiny chapel – the size perhaps of a small parish church – yet it is lined with 15 stained glass windows containing incredible colour and detail: there are over 1000 separate religious scenes depicted in all. Some 720 pieces of the glass are original, and are the oldest surviving stained glass in Paris – the chapel pre-dates Notre-Dame by almost 100 years. Sainte-Chapelle repays visiting at different times of day, and is well worth visiting towards sunset when the best feature of all, the 15th-century rose window in the rear of the chapel, may be illuminated by the gold of the setting sun. This contains 86 panels of glass, which tell the story of the Apocalypse.

Île St-Louis

The smaller of the two islands, Île St-Louis, is named after King Louis IX (1214–70), who used to enjoy its tranquillity as a place to say his prayers in the days when it was no more than a cow pasture. It isn't quite so peaceful these days, though much more so than its neighbour, the Île de la Cité, where the vast majority of visitors only stay long enough to see Notre-Dame and Sainte-Chapelle before going on their way again. Few bother to walk across the Pont St-Louis which joins the two islands, because Île St-Louis has no major tourist attraction – apart from itself.

Classical architecture

The island began to be developed in the early 17th century, and many of the Classical houses from that period survive, giving the island a consistent and pleasing look. Property is expensive, and appeals to those wealthy enough to buy it but who also like the fact that this still feels a little like the Paris of old, as you will appreciate from wandering round. The streets are narrow, the buildings often a few floors high on either side, making maximum use of the minimum space, and there is a definite sense of community – that people live here and shop here, like a little village in the centre of the city. There are plenty of shops and eating places, but only one school and one church on the island: the **Église St-Louis-en-l'Île**. This was built between 1664 and 1726, and has an ornate interior, which includes a plaque commemorating the fact that the St-Louis who gave his name to this island also provided the name for St Louis in Missouri.

The quais of the Seine

As well as exploring the back streets in the centre of the island – and there are plenty of great bars, restaurants and specialist shops just waiting to be discovered – take time to walk around the Quais that go around it. From the Quai d'Orléans on the southern side of the island to the west,

there is a great view of Notre-Dame and the Left Bank of the Seine, including the dome of the Panthéon, while the Quai de Bourbon at the northwest tip also has excellent views down the river.

Many famous people have lived on the island, including Camille Claudel (1864–1943), the sculptress and mistress of Rodin (her studio was at 19 Quai de Bourbon 1899–1913), Marie Curie (1867–1934), who lived at 36 Quai de Béthune, and the artist and caricaturist Honoré Daumier (1808–79), who lived at 9 Quai d'Anjou 1846–63.

Hôtel Lambert

Hôtel Lambert is the best-known house on the island, built in 1640 for a man known as Lambert the Rich and designed by Louis Le Vau, who lived on the island and also designed the Église St-Louis-en-l'Île as well as parts of the Louvre and Versailles. The house still contains many 17th-century treasures, and the elaborate ceilings rival and pre-date Le Vau's designs for the Great Hall of Mirrors at Versailles – but today the Hôtel is owned by the Rothschild family and is only occasionally opened to the public.

" Sometimes in the evening, sitting at ease alone on a bench on a boulevard, my mood would change. Free of glances which at home had the force of interdiction, released from the pressure of being known; the air perfumed with odours of flowers, dust and Gauloises, the pavements brimming with life that at midnight and beyond showed no signs of obeying any law of fatigue or any rule that things must come to an end, optimism was restored, and I remembered I had come to the right city. "

Peter Lennon,
Foreign Correspondent
(Picador, 1994)

81

Eating and Drinking

These are only two fairly small islands but the choice of eating and drinking places is large. On the Île de la Cité there are plenty of places producing cheap and fast food for the tourist market, while the Île St-Louis is the place to go for an authentic Parisian atmosphere and a good night out.

Cafés and Bars

Berthillon

31 Rue St-Louis-en-l'Île. Tel: 43 54 31 61. £. Ask any Parisian where you'll get the best ice-cream and the answer will be here, where they serve over 70 flavours (such as kiwi fruit, guava, whiskey, rhubarb, fig etc) in cones or tubs, to take away or eat on their own little terrace. *1000–2000 Wed–Sun.*

Taverne Henri IV

13 Place du Pont-Neuf. Tel: 43 54 27 90. ££. Long-established wine bar near the western tip of the Île de la Cité, usually packed with local workers there for the wine rather than the food, with plenty of choice by the glass. Food is served, with a regular *plat du jour* and plenty of snacks too, such as *charcuterie, escargots* and regional cheeses. *1200–2100 Mon–Fri, 1200–1600 Sat, food all day, closed Aug.*

Le Bar du Caveau

17 Place Dauphine. Tel: 43 54 45 95. ££. Right on the delightful Place Dauphine, this is a great place to sit and have lunch or while away the evening. It's popular with the people who live and work around here, and the occasional tourist who wanders through. There is a *plat du jour* and light snacks such as *charcuterie* and cheeses. *0830–2000 Mon–Fri and 1000–1900 Sat in May–July, food all day, closed two weeks in Aug, one week in Dec.*

Restaurants

Isami

4 Quai d'Orléans. Tel: 40 46 06 97. ££. It may seem strange to recommend a Japanese restaurant on Île St-Louis, but the sushi and sahimi here are terrific, and you can watch the chef prepare it all behind the counter. Stylish décor, fixed-price menus and à la carte, with more conventional seafood dishes too, such as sea bream – and the wine of course is French. *1200–1400 Tue–Sat and 1900–2230 Tue–Sun, closed two weeks in Aug.*

Brasserie de l'Île St-Louis

55 Quai de Bourbon. Tel: 43 54 02 59. ££. Great Parisian brasserie with the added setting of the island, and the buzz that creates. Always busy with locals and visitors alike. Serves food from Alsace, meaty regional fare: *charcuterie,* lamb, steaks, roast chicken. Nothing *nouvelle,* but satisfying and fabulous atmosphere – if you can get in. *1130–0130 Mon–Tue and Fri–Sun, 1800–0100 Thur. Closed Aug.*

Le Vieux Bistro

14 Rue du Cloître Notre-Dame. Tel: 43 54 18 95. £££. Immediately outside Notre-Dame and looks like a fairly ordinary bistro, but its comparatively high prices deter many tourists. This is a shame as price reflects quality, and this bistro is reckoned to serve the best *boeuf bourguignon* in Paris, amongst other things, such as Burgundy sausage, *civet de canard* (a thick duck stew), and a *tarte Tatin* (upside-down apple tart) flambéed in Calvados. *1200–1400 and 1930–2230 daily.*

Restaurant Paul

15 Place Dauphine. Tel: 43 54 21 48. ££. Wonderful setting in a Classical house set on this quiet square, this is a bustling bistro serving inexpensive and good-standard bistro grub: lobster salad, rack of lamb, chicken in tarragon sauce. A dessert speciality is *baba au rhum flambé. 1215–1430 and 1930–2230 daily.*

Clubs and nightlife

Not a nightclub area, the evening centres round eating – many of the restaurants and bars stay open just as late as on the Left Bank across the Seine.

Shopping

The islands are good for shopping, with lots of specialist shops in small premises – fashion, food and art in the main.

Boulangerie Rioux

35 Rue des Deux-Ponts. Tel: 43 54 57 59. Bread baked in their own wood-fired ovens. *Mon–Wed and Sat–Sun.*

Librairie Ulysse I

35 Rue St-Louis-en-l'Île. Tel: 43 25 17 35. Typical of an island shop: tiny, specialist with a knowledgeable owner. This specialises in travel books, in English and French. *1400–2000 Tue–Sat.*

Librairie Ulysse II

26 Rue St-Louis-en-l'Île. Tel: 43 29 52 10. The companion shop, stocking maps, travel magazines and books about France. *1400–2000 Tue–Sat.*

L'Épicerie

51 Rue St-Louis-en-l'Île. Tel: 43 25 20 14. Wonderful smells in this upmarket little food shop, where you will find a wide range of specialist jams, olive oils, vinegars, mustards, foie gras, sauces, teas, sweets and other treats for foodies. *1030–2000 daily.*

> " Mrs Allonby: *They say, Lady Hunstanton, that when good Americans die, they go to Paris.*
> Lady Hunstanton: *Indeed? And when bad Americans die, where do they go?*
> Lord Illingworth: *Oh, they go to America.* "
>
> **Oscar Wilde, *A Woman of No Importance***

The bridges of Paris

Everyone has heard the archetypal Parisian song 'Under the Bridges of Paris', and the bridges on the Seine – particularly those which link the two islands with the Left and Right banks and with each other – are well worth taking a close look at, either from below on the Quais if you can, or from up- or down-river on the neighbouring bridge.

The **Pont-Neuf** links the Île de la Cité with both the Left and Right banks, and despite its name meaning 'New Bridge' it is in fact the oldest surviving bridge in Paris. It was opened in 1607 when Henri IV (whose statue now stands on it) rode across it on horseback. It was also the first bridge in Paris which had a separate pavement for pedestrians, and the first to be built without houses on it. This point at the western tip of the island, where the Seine reunites after flowing around it, is where the river is at its widest – a width that is spanned by 12 arches. It was built in two halves and isn't in fact perfectly straight.

New, old and rebuilt

The **Pont St-Michel** was first built in 1378, though the
present construction dates from 1857, while the **Petit Pont**, or
Little Bridge, is also a 19th-century replacement for an earlier
bridge. That one was first built in 1185 by Bishop Maurice
de Sully, who was involved in the building of Notre-Dame
and after whom the **Pont de Sully** is named – the bridge
which crosses the eastern end of Île St-Louis. The bridge
linking the two islands is the pedestrianised **Pont St-Louis**,
the current one being the ninth to bridge this narrow crossing.
The first went up in 1634 and came down the same day,
drowning 20 people. The **Pont Marie**, between the Île
St-Louis and the Right Bank, was opened in 1635, but in 1658
was partly swept away in a flood, destroying 22 of the houses
which stood on it and killing 121 people. Perhaps 'Under the
Bridges of Paris' is not the best place to be, after all.

Les Halles, Marais and Bastille

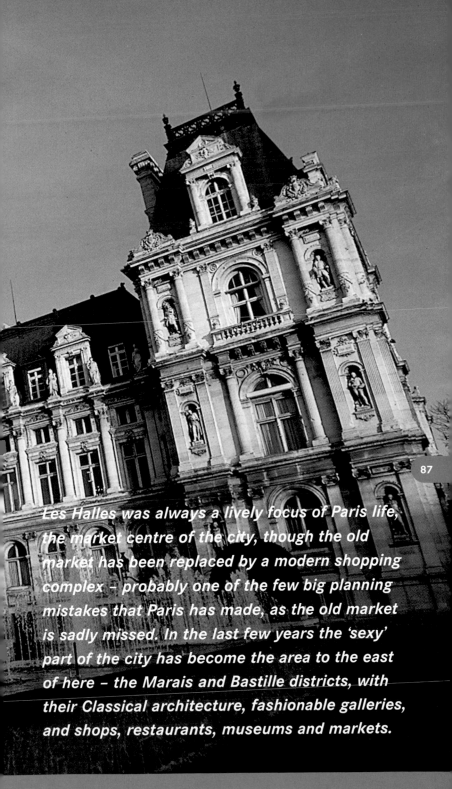

Les Halles was always a lively focus of Paris life, the market centre of the city, though the old market has been replaced by a modern shopping complex – probably one of the few big planning mistakes that Paris has made, as the old market is sadly missed. In the last few years the 'sexy' part of the city has become the area to the east of here – the Marais and Bastille districts, with their Classical architecture, fashionable galleries, and shops, restaurants, museums and markets.

LES HALLES, MARAIS AND BASTILLE

Getting there: **Métro:** *Place de la Bastille has its own station, as does Les Halles; St-Paul is best for the Marais.* **RER:** *Châtelet Les Halles for Les Halles; no RER in the Marais district.* **Buses:** *Bastille 20, 29, 65, 69, 76, 86, 87, 91; Place des Vosges 20, 29, 69, 76, 96; Musée Picasso 29, 96; Les Halles 29, 38, 47, 74.*

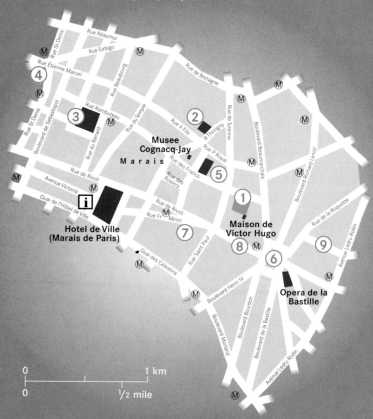

LES HALLES, MARAIS AND BASTILLE

① Walk round the Place des Vosges

This is the oldest square in Paris, and also considered to be one of its prettiest, with arcades lining all four sides and a pleasant fountain-filled park in the centre. Here youngsters play in the evening, watched by the old folk, none of them caring two hoots that the place is now fashionable. **Pages 100–101**

② Don't miss the Musée Picasso

Housed in a beautiful mansion, worth seeing in its own right, this is a tribute to the genius and the prolific nature of the man who was probably the 20th century's greatest artist. The collection is based round the works he wanted to keep for himself rather than put up for sale. **Pages 96–97**

③ Centre Beaubourg (Pompidou Centre)

It outrages many people, for its modernistic 'inside-out' design, but that doesn't stop it being the most-visited attraction in Paris – amazingly it gets more visitors than even the Louvre and the Eiffel Tower. You can't miss it – in more ways than one. **Pages 92–93**

④ Get lost in the Forum des Halles

This huge multi-story, partly underground modern shopping centre, combining a Métro and RER station as well, is a vast complex of stores and escalators, with much-needed maps at every corner. You're sure to get lost at some point – just getting in and out is a challenge – but shopaholics won't mind in the least! **Pages 102–103**

⑤ See the Musée Carnavalet

An eclectic collection of fine art objects, paintings, statues, murals and models of the city, all contained in one of the Marais' grand 16th-century mansion houses. Fascinating glimpses of the changing – and unchanging – face of the city. **Pages 98–99**

⑥ See the Place de la Bastille

It's noisy and it's filled with traffic, but it's also a square on a grand scale, with great historical resonance, and the hub for an area that is up-and-coming and should be on every visitor's list. **Pages 90–91**

⑦ Visit the Maison Européenne de la Photographie

Paris is not just a city for the holiday snapper, it has both produced and inspired many of the world's greatest photographers. This new exhibition space on several floors celebrates some of the best photography, old and new. **Page 99**

⑧ Go shopping for food

No shortage of food shops in the Marais, especially on Rue St-Antoine; the markets around Place de la Bastille are among the best in the city. **Pages 91 and 94**

⑨ Eat on Rue de Lappe one night

This boisterous street is lined with eating and drinking places, from brash fast-food joints to places for people with more refined palates. If you're stuck for somewhere to eat, Rue de Lappe is bound to provide something – not least the nightlife atmosphere. **Pages 91, 104–105**

Place de la Bastille

The Bastille Prison is what stood in the centre of the huge Place de la Bastille – not the most attractive of Paris's many grand places but still impressive with the Colonne de Juillet in the centre of the heavy traffic flow. The bronze column, with its golden statue on top, is 52m (171ft) high and commemorates the Parisians who died in uprisings in 1830 and 1848, and before that the storming of the Bastille itself on 14 July 1789, after which the mob tore down the hated fortress prison.

Today the whole Bastille area is being regenerated and has become fashionable – Jean-Paul Gaultier has opened a shop nearby – in the way that had previously happened to the neighbouring district of the Marais. Roads radiate out from the Bastille like spokes on a wheel, and it is Rue St-Antoine that leads west to the Marais (*see pages 94–95*). Number 5 Rue St-Antoine was the actual site of the Bastille's courtyard, where the crowd broke into the prison. On the north side of the Place is the **Opéra-Bastille**, the largest opera house in the world and a building hated by many for being too overblown, though it has no doubt helped play its part in the regeneration of this area.

South from the Bastille is the Canal St-Martin, constructed in 1821 to enable supplies to be taken into and out of the factories and warehouses in the Faubourg St-Antoine district. Walk east from the Place down **Rue du Faubourg St-Antoine** and

> " *Now, hip Paris has descended en masse into the Bastille, once a poor, working-class neighbourhood. New bars and restaurants are opening every week, fashion boutiques are replacing outdated furniture shops, and back-street artisan's ateliers are transformed into trendy lofts or minimalist art galleries.* "
>
> **John Brunton, *Daily Telegraph*, 4 Dec 1998**

you will see some of these old factories, mostly for furniture, which are now being transformed into units for art galleries and smaller craftsmen's workshops as the area has been 'trendified'. Many of these are in small alleyways and courtyards off the street, such as the Cour de l'Étoile d'Or and the Passage du Chantier – a cobbled passageway with a concentration of furniture makers. Fashion designer Jean-Paul Gaultier has his discreet shopfront at number 30, hiding his often less-than-discreet clothing.

Markets

North from Place de la Bastille runs the wide **Boulevard Richard-Lenoir**, down the centre of which is one of the city's best produce markets, on Thursday and Sunday mornings. It is especially busy on Sundays, and quickly becomes packed with buyers and browsers alike, so try and get there before about 1000 if you want to have chance to look around. There are cheese stalls, honey stalls, stalls specialising in shellfish, bread, wine or in produce from different regions of France – irresistible smells and colours. At the far end of the boulevard, as you approach the Place de la République, is another food market, the Popincourt Market, on Tuesday and Friday mornings. Three different markets also cluster together around Place d'Aligre, just off the Rue du Faubourg St-Antoine, every morning except Monday. There is a smart and expensive covered market where you can buy fine wines and cheeses, game, even truffles, while outside is a cheaper food market, and also a bric-a-brac market: clothes, tools, books and general junk.

Cafés and nightlife

Off to the right, just north of Place de la Bastille along Boulevard Richard-Lenoir, is **Rue de Lappe**. Almost every building in this narrow street seems to be a bar, restaurant, café or club, and at night it positively throbs with music and is jammed with crowds, all checking out where to eat, drink or simply be seen. Whether you want pre-dinner drinks, dinner, a nightcap, or all of them and more, Rue de Lappe can provide it.

Centre Beaubourg (Pompidou Centre)

*With its 'inside-out' architecture incorporating highly-visible and garishly-coloured pipes, which make it look as if it's been partly built out of Lego, the **Centre Beaubourg** (or Pompidou Centre, as it is more popularly known in English) has become as much a Paris landmark as the Eiffel Tower or the Louvre Pyramid. There is no other building in the world like it – and thank goodness, its critics would no doubt say. Its brash approach does appeal, however, and it is the most-visited place in Paris. 1200–2200 Mon and Wed–Fri, 1000–2200 Sat–Sun. Free for Centre but admission charge to exhibitions.*

It has had slightly fewer visitors recently while parts have been closed for renovation, timed to reopen to coincide with the Millennium celebrations. One of its main attractions was the **Musée National d'Art Moderne** (National Museum of Modern Art), part of which has been loaned out to the Palais de Tokyo (*see pages 26–27*) but will be re-housed here in new galleries which, if past experience is anything to go by, will be something quite special.

The building

The idea for a multi-purpose modern art centre was set in motion by President Pompidou in 1969, but not completed until 1977, three years after his death. The design is by the English architect Richard Rogers (who also designed the Lloyd's Building in London) and the Italian Renzo Piano. Having water, electricity and other pipes outside the building (the pipes you see do serve a practical purpose) frees up more space inside for exhibitions. In addition to the National Museum of Modern Art, which the visitor is most likely to see, the Centre also contains the largest public library in Paris, covering three floors and providing access to half a million books as well as videos, films, magazines, photographs and CD-ROMs. The Grande Galerie on the 5th floor is used for temporary exhibitions, and there are always buskers and other forms of street theatre in the large open area outside.

Near the Centre

There are two modern sculptures near the Centre which shouldn't be missed – indeed, one of them can hardly be missed, being as distinctive in its own way as the Centre itself. The Fontaine de Stravinsky is a fantasy fountain inspired by Stravinsky's ballet *The Firebird*. It was designed by Niki de Saint-Phalle and Jean Tinguely, the latter a French artist very much inspired by Pop Art. The fountain is a colourful piece of fun, with jets of water firing out, turning sculptures and the Firebird itself in the middle of it all.

> " I often write at the Café Beaubourg, which strikes the English, who love crowded, smoky pubs, as disagreeably austere and new, but which I find airy and calm although there's always something to see. It was built at the end of the 1980s, right across from the Centre Georges Pompidou and the giant digital clock that counts down the seconds that remain until the end of the century. "
>
> **Edmund White, from**
> ***Our Paris: Sketches***
> ***from Memory***

In the shopping centre called the Quartier de l'Horloge, just to the north of the Centre, is another futuristic fantasy piece of sculpture, the Defender of Time. This one-ton sculpture by Jacques Monestier comes to life on the hour, every hour. The warrior whose job it is to defend time is attacked by one of the creatures around him (bird, crab or dragon), fending them off with his sword. At noon, 1800 and 2200, all three creatures attack in a clash of metal and jerking movements. It won't detain you for long, but it's fun while it lasts.

93

The Marais

The Marais today is one of the most fashionable areas of Paris, and among the most popular with visitors – though it wasn't always the collection of Classical buildings and glitzy galleries that it is now. The French word marais *means 'marsh', and that's exactly what it was until the 13th century, when the Knights Templar, who had occupied the north of this district (still known today as Temple), began draining the swamps that lay between them and the River Seine to the south.*

Further development took place when King Henry IV took a shine to the area at the start of the 17th century, particularly with the creation of the Place des Vosges (*see pages 100–101*), which was and remains one of the city's most beautiful squares. Many of the grand houses which went up during this period of development still remain, some turned into museums, others into offices and tasteful apartment blocks. It all makes for a great area to wander around, with no shortage of good eating and drinking places too.

Food shops in Rue St-Antoine

The main street, with the St-Paul Métro stop, is **Rue St-Antoine**. Food shoppers should walk along here towards Place de la Bastille, as it contains many first-class shops, some specialising in cheeses, others in patisseries or produce from a particular region – there is even a horse-meat shop, and there aren't too many of those left in Paris these days.

The other main street to see is the **Rue des Francs-Bourgeois**, along which are many of the fine old houses. They include the Palais Soubise, home of the Archives de France, which contains important historical documents such as letters by Joan of Arc and Voltaire, Napoléon's will, a copy of the Declaration of the Rights of Man and an estimated further six billion documents. Also in this street is the Hôtel Lamoignon, a splendid early-17th-century mansion which now houses the Bibliothèque Historique de la Ville de Paris, the city's historical library.

The Jewish Quarter

The Marais has always had its **Jewish Quarter**, which centres on the Rue des Rosiers (Street of the Rosebushes), with its kosher butchers, delis, bakers and bookshops. It has been Jewish since the marshes were first drained, suffered terrible losses during World War II, when an estimated 75,000 Jews were taken to the extermination camps, was regenerated by the arrival of North African Jews after the war, but has suffered again more recently at the hands – and occasional bombs – of France's right-wing Front National.

Gay Paris

The Marais has also become the **gay centre** of Paris, based on and around the Rue Ste-Croix-de-la-Bretonnerie, where there are gay businesses and co-operatives, shops with names like Boy'z Bazaar, and even gay libraries. If you are in Paris for Bastille Day, then watch out for the gay and lesbian Bastille Day Ball, which starts at 2200 on 13 July and continues through the night on Quai de la Tournelle on the Left Bank.

> **"** *The last time I saw Paris, her heart was warm and gay,*
> *I heard the laughter of her heart in every street café.* **"**
>
> **Oscar Hammerstein II, 'The Last Time I Saw Paris' from *Lady Be Good***

Musée Picasso

*The **Musée Picasso** (Picasso Museum), also sometimes called the Hôtel Salé after the mansion which houses it, is the other 'must see' site in the Marais along with the Place des Vosges (0915–1715 Thur–Mon, 0915–2200 Wed). The house itself was built between 1656 and 1659 for a salt tax collector, which is how it gets its name. It was an art school until 1969, when it was closed and refurbished to open as this splendid museum, dedicated to the work of Spanish-born but long-time Paris resident Pablo Picasso (1881–1973), considered by many to be the great art genius of the 20th century.*

Picasso

Picasso was born in Málaga and studied in both Barcelona and Madrid before coming to Paris, the centre of the art world. He lived at 7 Rue des Grands Augustins in St-Germain from 1936 until 1955, and it was there he painted what is perhaps his best-known work amongst many: *Guernica*. That is not on display here (it is in the Reina Sofia Art Centre in Madrid), but what is here is a unique collection by the standards of any artist, let alone the versatile and prolific Picasso.

When the artist died in 1973, his heirs gave large parts of his private collection to the French State in lieu of death duties. What is interesting about Picasso's collection is that quite early on in his career, once he was financially secure, he limited the number of paintings he sold and kept his personal favourites for himself. He also kept hold of the works he happened to be painting during the week of his birthday, 25 October. Together these make up quite simply the largest collection of Picassos in the world. In addition he amassed a large collection of work by contemporaries he admired or befriended, including Cézanne, Rousseau, Braque, Matisse and Renoir. In all there are almost 4000 pieces, including 200 paintings, sculptures, ceramics, over 3000 drawings, collages, prints and sketchbooks, enhanced by photographs of the artist – including many light-hearted personal ones with friends and family – and video displays of him working, as well as occasional temporary exhibitions of his work from elsewhere.

> " Sometimes in the evening, sitting at ease alone on a bench on a boulevard, my mood would change. Free of glances which at home had the force of interdiction, released from the pressure of being known; the air perfumed with odours of flowers, dust and Gauloises, the pavements brimming with life that at midnight and beyond showed no signs of obeying any law of fatigue or any rule that things must come to an end, optimism was restored, and I remembered I had come to the right city. "

Peter Lennon,
Foreign Correspondent
(Picador, 1994)

Blue nudes and cubes

The work is arranged chronologically through the slightly maze-like mansion, and illustrates the artist's energy as well as ability to diversify into many different fields, and his sheer talent at seemingly mastering any style or technique he attempted. His Blue Period is well represented, and the basement area contains a large collection of his lesser-known sculptures. There are large numbers of nudes and Cubist works, and a tender portrait of his son, Paul, dressed as a harlequin. His first-ever collage, *Still Life with Chair Caning*, which he produced in 1912 just before moving on to experiment with Cubism. There is also an excellent little gift shop containing fairly tasteful artistic souvenirs of work by Picasso and other artists.

Marais museums

The Marais has many other museums, large and small, though some probably appeal only to the specialist, such as the museums devoted to dolls, to hunting or to locks. On Place des Vosges there is the Musée Victor Hugo (see page 101).

City of Paris Historical Museum

A major collection which is of interest to anyone interested in Paris is held at the **Hôtel et Musée Carnavalet**, also known as the **Musée Historique de la Ville de Paris** at 23 Rue de Sévigné (*1000–1740 Tue–Wed and Fri–Sun, 1000–2030 Thur*). This collection is housed in yet another fine Marais mansion, which was begun in 1548 to a design by Pierre Lescot (who also designed the Louvre), has some later additions (notably the 19th-century wings surrounding its three courtyards), and has housed the museum since 1880. It is an eclectic collection, covering all types of arts and crafts, all combining to tell the history of Paris between 1500 and 1900. Of particular interest are the many paintings which show the changing face of the city, especially on the Seine, where older bridges lined with wooden houses have been destroyed by fires and replaced by newer designs. On the second floor are special displays on the events and personalities of the French Revolution.

Musée Cognacq-Jay

Much smaller but also worth seeing is the **Musée Cognacq-Jay** at 8 Rue Elzévir (*1000–1740 Tue–Sun*). The names refer to Ernest Cognacq and his wife Louise Jay, who amassed this private collection of 18th-century art through their wealth from having founded the Samaritaine department store. Cognacq left it to the State when he died in 1928. It is displayed in the 16th-century Hôtel Donon, which if not from the exact period of its contents is at least a fitting setting for them, with much wood-panelling and tastefully-lit display cases. There are drawings and paintings by Watteau, Rembrandt, Fragonard, Gainsborough, Reynolds and Canaletto, amongst others, comprising not a huge collection but still an impressive one. In addition there are ceramics, Meissen porcelain, sculptures, jewellery and furniture.

European Photography Gallery

More modern is the **Maison Européenne de la Photographie** (European Photography Gallery) at 5–7 Rue de Fourcy (*1100–2000 Wed–Sun*). This EU initiative was opened in 1996 in an 18th-century mansion with a modern extension which could not be more different yet somehow looks right. The Gallery has a permanent collection of some 12,000 photographs, although obviously not all are on permanent display. The exhibitions vary, with rotating examples of work from the permanent collection, combined with visiting exhibitions and displays relating to the work of French photographers such as Cartier-Bresson (*see pages 162–163*). What does not vary are the beautiful light galleries in the warren-like building, which also has video display areas, a delightful basement café and a small bookshop. Also in the basement area are mixed media and more experimental displays, and while these change regularly the visitor can be assured of a stimulating time in this enjoyable building.

> **"** We work in unison with movement as though it were a presentiment of the way life itself unfolds. But inside movement there is one moment at which the elements in motion are in balance. Photography must seize upon this moment and hold immobile the equilibrium of it. **"**
>
> **Henri Cartier-Bresson, *The Decisive Moment* (1952)**

Place des Vosges

The oldest square in Paris goes back to 1612, when it was completed on the orders of King Henri IV, who had decided to turn the Marais into one of the best areas in Paris (see page 94) with a beautiful and symmetrical square at its heart. All the buildings were to be built in harmony with each other – an effect that was majestically achieved, as can be seen today just as well as almost 400 years ago. It was known then as the Place Royale, but after the Revolution became the Place de l'Indivisibilité and finally in 1800 the Place des Vosges, after the Vosges region of northeast France (the first to pay up the newly introduced taxes).

Though the square seems large there are in fact only 36 buildings around the four sides, none more than three floors high and all linked with galleried arcades – the first time houses in Paris were linked in this way. It is as exquisite a place for shopping and strolling as it was when it was built, when it was *the* place to live and to parade around. The south side is dominated by the largest single building, **Le Pavillon du Roi** (King's Pavilion), opposite which is **Le Pavillon de la Reine** (Queen's Pavilion). This northern side of the square is today filled with art galleries, from the traditional to the avant-garde. Other sides of the square have more galleries, fashionable clothes shops (Issey Miyake is at number 3), chic cafés and, in the southeast corner, the house in which Victor Hugo lived from 1833 until 1848.

Victor Hugo's house

The **Maison de Victor Hugo** (*6 Place des Vosges; 1000–1740 Tue–Sun*) is in the Hôtel de Rohan-Guéménée. Hugo (1802–85) became the greatest French novelist of the 19th century, and only left this elegant home in 1848, when Napoléon III took power and Hugo's increasing involvement in the politics of the day forced him to flee, initially to Belgium and then in 1855 to a 15-year exile on Guernsey. His home on the island is strongly featured here, with many photos both of it and of the writer and his family there. The collection of mementoes and artefacts shows Hugo's great interest in photography, and his own ability as an artist as well as a wordsmith. Hugo's desk is here, along with letters and other documents, editions of his books, a strong Rodin bust of the author, and not least a lovely view of the Place des Vosges from the upstairs windows.

" *The Parisian is to the French what the Athenian was to the Greeks: no one sleeps better than he, no one is more openly frivolous and idle, no one appears more heedless. But this is misleading. He is given to every kind of listlessness, but when there is glory to be won he may be inspired with every kind of fury. Give him a pike and he will enact the tenth of August, a musket and you have Austerlitz. He was the springboard of Napoleon and the mainstay of Danton. At the cry of 'la patrie' he enrols, and at the call of liberty he tears up the pavements. Beware of him!* "

Victor Hugo, *Les Misérables* (1862)

Other notable houses on the square include number 1, where Madame de Sévigné (1626–96) was born. Her published collection of over 1500 letters was a literary triumph when it appeared, and gives a detailed and very intimate account of courtly life in the 17th century. Cardinal Richelieu lived at number 21 Place des Vosges (1615–27), as did the writer Molière. In the southwest corner of the Place is the Hôtel de Sully, which houses the government offices for the Bureau of Historic Monuments and Sites. You can walk through its courtyard, which links the Place des Vosges with the Rue St-Antoine in a delightful short-cut.

Les Halles

It was at the start of the 12th century when the main Paris market was transferred to Les Halles, so little wonder there was uproar when it was relocated to the outskirts of the city almost 900 years later. Not enough uproar, however, to save the old market, which was described by Émile Zola as 'The Belly of Paris' (in his novel of that title Le Ventre de Paris*), and which also featured in Victor Hugo's novel* Les Misérables. *Nearby were the courtyards he referred to as the 'Miracle Courtyards', because it was here that the blind and crippled beggars who hung round the markets used to live, becoming miraculously cured as soon as they returned home.*

In the mid 19th century, ten market halls were built of girders and glass, setting the style for covered markets throughout Europe. By the 1960s, however, it was felt that they were too small to contain the ever-increasing market trade, especially in the very centre of Paris, so they were moved out to the district of Rungis near Orly Airport in 1969 and replaced ten years later with the **Forum des Halles**.

Bordellos

The area around Les Halles gave the world the word 'bordello'. To shelter from the rain the working girls used to make huts from wooden boards, **bordes**, *and hence bordellos. The huts have gone but in that area some of the bordellos live on.*

The Forum shopping centre

The Forum is an ambitious shopping complex which stretches over 17 acres, although 12 acres consist of gardens (Jardin des Halles). At the base of the Forum is the world's biggest and busiest underground train station, combining as it does both Métro and RER station (the linked Les Halles and Châtelet Les Halles.) There are several floors, both above and below ground, with shops, 12 restaurants, countless bars and cafés, cinemas and galleries. The attempt to civilise this cathedral of consumerism by the inclusion of art and poetry pavilions has been somewhat hampered by the fact that they are difficult to find among the miles of walkways, lifts, escalators and location maps. Nevertheless, the Forum des Halles is something to be experienced, if not necessarily enjoyed.

For more sophisticated shopping, walk the short distance to the **Place des Victoires** – a circle of distinguished town houses which have become a focus for high-fashion shops, notably Kenzo, Thierry Mugler, Cacharel, Agatha and even Miki House for designer-conscious children.

Église St-Eustache

Between the Forum des Halles and Place des Victoires stands the unmistakable massive shape of the **Église St-Eustache**, the parish church of the Les Halles district and regarded as one of the most beautiful churches in the city. This Gothic giant was begun in 1532 but not completed until 1637. It is 105m (346ft) long with a neck-aching nave that towers up to 34m (112ft). There are many frescoes and sculptures, an early painting by Rubens (*The Pilgrims at Emmaus*), and a highly appropriate sculpture commemorating the market traders of the Les Halles of old. St-Eustache is also notable for its musical links, as Berlioz's *Te Deum* and Liszt's *Grand Mass* both had their first public performances here. Concerts are still held in the church, so look out for details, particularly if they feature the church's 8000-pipe organ.

Eating and drinking

A great area for good food, particularly these days around the Bastille and north towards Place de la République. The Marais, being popular now with tourists, has no shortage of places to eat and drink, but the best restaurants are often just away from the fashionable areas, where rents can quickly escalate.

Cafés and Bars

Le Béarn

9 Rue de Béarn. Tel: 42 72 78 64. £. A long-established plain and simple café/bar in the Marais, handy for Place des Vosges and serving hearty Lyonnais food as well as wine by the glass, beer and coffee. *0700–1900 Mon–Fri, food all day, closed Aug.*

Café des Musées

49 Rue de Turenne. Tel: 42 72 96 17. £. Well-located for the Marais museums and Place des Vosges, a smart corner café which also serves sandwiches, salads and simple meals. *0700–2300 Mon–Sat, 0800–2000 Sun, food from noon.*

Café des Phares

7 Place de la Bastille. Tel: 42 72 04 70. £. Only in Paris: this place is turned into an intellectual debating chamber on Sunday lunchtimes by philosopher and Sorbonne lecturer Marc Sautet. However, you can have a coffee or a snack, and contemplate the meaning of life by yourself, almost all day, every day. *0700–0400 daily, food 0930–0300.*

Restaurants

Chez Georges

1 Rue du Mail. Tel: 42 60 07 11. £££. No *nouvelle cuisine* here – more old-world cuisine, but extremely well-done. This long-established bistro appeals to the well-heeled bourgeoisie who live and work nearby, hence some wines which would require a mortgage, though there are cheaper options to accompany traditional bistro fare such as duck with mushrooms, hefty steaks, grilled fish. Don't let simplicity deceive – it's top-notch food and a great old-fashioned atmosphere. *1200–1400 and 1900–2130 Mon–Sat, closed three weeks in Aug.*

Au Pied de Cochon

6 Rue Coquillière. Tel: 40 13 77 00. ££. A name that means 'At the Pig's Foot' suggests basic hearty grub, and that's what you get at this revered old brasserie that made its name catering to the robust appetites of the market traders at nearby Les Halles (and getting the best cuts of meat in return). You don't have to have pig's trotter, though the other dish which it's famed for is onion soup, a warming winter restorative. It's equally known for fish and shellfish too. *Open 24 hours, daily.*

L'Escargot Montorgueil

38 Rue Montorgueil. Tel: 42 36 83 51.
££. Worth it for the 1820s décor, and an essential visit if you happen to like snails, which merit their own mini-menu: with mint, curried, with garlic, with Roquefort butter etc. There are non-escargot options such as steaks, roast duck, rack of lamb, marinated salmon, and an indication of the clientele is that they serve champagne by the carafe. *1200–1400 and 1930–2300 daily.*

La Galoche d'Aurillac

41 Rue de Lappe. Tel: 47 00 77 15. ££.
A very lively Auvergnat restaurant on this street of eateries. A front bar where locals pop in for a drink, and a restaurant at rear and downstairs serving generous quantities of tasty Auvergnat fare: hams, sausages, duck, steaks, stuffed veal. Bring a meaty appetite. *1200–1430 and 1900–2330 Tue–Sat, closed Aug.*

Les Sans-Culottes

27 Rue de Lappe. Tel: 48 05 42 92.
££. Relaxed bistro atmosphere, equally popular with tourists and young Parisians for its economical fixed-price menu and wider *à la carte* options, such as veal kidneys with wild mushrooms, duck in raspberry sauce, and grilled salmon with garlic and basil sauce. An authentic old feel to it – even if it was only built recently! *1200–1445 and 1900–2400 Tue–Sun.*

Au C'Amelot

50 Rue Amelot. Tel: 43 55 54 04. ££.
Slightly north of the Marais but worth the short journey for a unique dining experience: a fixed-price set menu of five courses, your only choice being which of the excellent puddings to have, and which wine to choose from a wide and not expensive list. Main course dictated by what's fresh in the market, and it may be venison or wild boar in a plum and honey sauce. Book ahead at busy times. *1200–1430 and 1900–2200 Mon–Sat, closed Aug.*

> " *Marc Sautet recently opened France's first philosophy practice, where patients can shed their metaphysical angst rather as they might try to shed more mundane forms of angst at the psychiatrist's. What is the purpose of human existence? What is existence? Does existence exist? For a fee, Sautet will discuss all this and more in a one-to-one conversation in his office at the end of a dark corridor in the Marais district.* "

Adam Sage, 'French Revolutionaries Chew the Fat in Cafés', *Observer*

Clubs and nightlife

Café Concert Ailleurs

13 Rue Jean-Beausire. Tel: 44 59 82 82. ££. This café hosts live concerts nightly at 2100, which could be anything from poetry readings to comics to traditional French chansons, so check local listings for details. *1830–0100 daily, food till midnight, closed Aug.*

China Club

50 Rue de Charenton. Tel: 43 43 82 02. £££. Absolutely *the* place to see and be seen if you know that Bastille is now fashionable. Have a pre- or post-dinner drink in one of the several bars – the Chinese/French food is OK, but most people drift out to eat and then drift back later. *1900–0200 Mon–Thur, 1900–0300 Fri–Sat, food 1930–0030.*

Lizard Lounge

18 Rue du Bourg-Tibourg. Tel: 42 72 81 34. Open all day, but the cellar bar has DJs every night pulling in a young hip crowd. Snacks and main meals are served from about noon until 2230. *1100–0200 daily.*

Le Balajo

9 Rue de Lappe. Tel: 47 00 07 87. ££. This Latin club dishes up a range of music including Cuban and rock on different nights, so check local listings. *2300–0500 Mon, Thur–Sat, 2100–0200 Wed, 1500–1830 Sun.*

What's Up Bar

15 Rue Daval. Tel: 48 05 88 33. £. Whatever's happening in music, it's usually happening here, being listened to and danced to by a hip young crowd. Many from the music business come to check things out. *1830–0200 Sun–Thur, 2200–0500 Fri–Sat.*

Shopping

agnès b

3 Rue du Jour. Tel: 44 39 02 60. A chic French chain of shops providing stylish contemporary fashions, this one close by Forum des Halles. *Mon–Sat.*

Legrand

1 Rue de la Banque. Tel: 42 60 07 12. Épicerie with an especially good wine selection alongside the best jams, mustards, olive oil, tea, coffee – and chocolate. *Tue–Sat.*

Izraël

30 Rue François-Miron. Tel: 42 72 66 23. Wonderful specialist food shop stocking herbs, spices, nibbles and booze from around the world. Worth calling in just to sniff around, even if you don't want to buy. *0930–1300 and 1430–1600 Tue–Fri, 0930–1600 Sat, closed Aug.*

Rue Montorgueil Market

For a flavour of old Les Halles visit this street market nearby where many people – including local restaurateurs – continue to shop, and savour the scene in one of the several pavement cafés. *Mornings Tue–Sun.*

Markets: *see also page 91* under **Place de la Bastille.**

Writers in Paris, and Paris in print

Paris and literature go together just as readily as Paris

and romance or Paris and art. Names such as Voltaire, Victor Hugo and inevitably Hemingway are as much a part of the city's history as any number of physical monuments. You could soak yourself in the city's atmosphere by doing some advance reading, though a full list of books about the city would fill a shop let alone a shelf.

Hemingway's *A Moveable Feast* is essential reading, as the author concentrates less on his hard-bitten style and more on an affectionate portrait of a city of starving authors when he was there in the early 1920s. Still starving a decade later, the carnal side of the city was captured by Henry Miller in *Tropic of Cancer* and the later *Quiet Days in Clichy*.

Colette, Hugo and Zola

The seedy, sleazy, run-down side of the city has been
documented by Colette in her many memoirs and semi-
autobiographical novels set in Paris, such as *Les Claudine*,
a series of four novels which recount the growing up of
Claudine/Colette at the turn of the century, and *Gigi*, later
turned into a famous film musical starring Maurice Chevalier.
Also turned into a musical of a rather different kind was
Victor Hugo's *Les Misérables*, which details the sufferings
of the poor in Paris in the early years of the 19th century.
The *Hunchback of Notre Dame* deals with medieval Paris
and the unforgettable love story between Quasimodo and
Esmerelda. Paris-born Émile Zola is another French novelist
who has chronicled the sufferings of the poor, and deals
with Paris in *Le Ventre de Paris* and *Thérèse Raquin*,
amongst others.

Low-life and crime

More low-life is vividly described by George Orwell in one
of his finest works of non-fiction, *Down and Out in Paris
and London*, a 1930s portrait of what went on beyond the
kitchen door in restaurants. More recently the Maigret
detective novels of Georges Simenon centre round the police
headquarters on the Île de la Cité, while the American
novelist James Baldwin's *Giovanni's
Room* is set in 1950s
homosexual
Paris, a world
also explored by
the American
writer Edmund
White, who has
made Paris his
home and described
it in his non-fiction
book *Our Paris:
Sketches from Memory*.

St-Honoré

This is glitzy Paris, the Paris of the Hôtel Ritz and designer shops whose names are a roll-call of haute couture: Gaultier, Gucci, Ungaro, Dior, Courrèges, Guy Laroche, Pierre Cardin, Hermès and Yves Saint-Laurent. It is the Paris which appeals to the gourmand as well as to the fashion-fiend, and a shop-window stroll round Place de la Madeleine will show why: truffles and champagne is just the start of it. It's the Paris of the Opéra, the Palais Royal and the Palais de l'Élysée, where the President of France lives. And if it's good enough for the President, it's certainly good enough to warrant a few hours of window-shopping at the very least.

ST-HONORÉ

BEST OF
St-Honoré

Getting there: **Métro:** *Opéra for Place de l'Opéra and Place Vendôme; Madeleine for Place de la Madeleine and Rue du Faubourg St-Honoré; Palais Royal–Musée du Louvre for Palais Royal.* **RER:** *none in this area.* **Buses:** *Opéra area 20, 21, 22, 27, 29, 42, 52, 53, 66, 68, 81, 95; Rue du Faubourg St-Honoré 24, 28, 32, 42, 49, 52, 80, 83, 84, 94; Place de la Madeleine 24, 42, 52, 84, 94; Palais Royal 21, 27, 39, 48, 67, 69, 72, 81, 85, 95.*

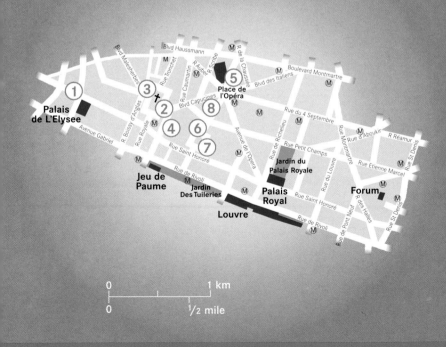

① See the chic shops of Rue du Faubourg St-Honoré

Even the dogs are likely to be fashionably dressed here, where women in expensive furs stroll snootily around and every other shop has a world-famous name. This is the heart of Gold Card and Gucci country, worth seeing even if all you can afford is a Gucci handkerchief. **Pages 114–115**

② Shop for food on Place de la Madeleine

If you can walk by the food displays at a shop like Fauchon without wanting to stop and buy half the window, then you're in the wrong city. The square also has bakers and chocolate shops, and other stylish displays to make you drool. **Pages 116–117**

③ See the Église Ste-Marie Madeleine

Built like a Greek temple, this startlingly unusual church almost overwhelms the square in which it stands, as if it had taken a holiday from Athens and got lost. **Pages 116–117**

④ Use the public loo at Place de la Madeleine

If you have to go, or even if you don't, head for this 1905 Art Nouveau public toilet with its stained glass and wood panelling, below the street on the south side of Place de la Madeleine. In St-Honoré, even the toilets are chic.

⑤ Have a night at the Opéra, without seeing an opera

All operas now take place at the new Opéra-Bastille (*see page 90*) but the Opéra-Garnier here, once the largest in the world, still stages the best of ballet and modern dance. **Pages 122–123**

⑥ Take in the elegant Place Vendôme

With Cartier in one corner, Armani in another and the Hôtel Ritz dominating one side, the spacious Place Vendôme joins the precious élite of grand Parisian squares. **Pages 118–119**

⑦ Have a drink at the Ritz ...

You may not be able to afford to stay in the hotel, but a drink in the Ritz Bar allows you to join names such as Ernest Hemingway, President Roosevelt, Noel Coward and Greta Garbo, who have all relaxed here with a glass – or two. **Pages 118–119**

⑧ ... and a second in Harry's Bar

Another watering hole for the rich and famous, and the not-so-rich and not-so-famous too. It's the place where they invented the Bloody Mary as a hangover cure, the need for which has never gone out of fashion. **Page 124**

113

> " Her frocks are built in Paris but she wears them with a strong English accent. "
>
> **Saki (British writer Hector Hugh Munro, 1870–1916),** *Reginald on Women*

Rue du Faubourg St-Honoré

This fashionable address runs all the way from near Place de la Madeleine out to Place des Ternes in northwest Paris, almost reaching the Boulevard Périphérique, but it is the eastern end which has become one of the most chic shopping streets in the world.

From Place de la Madeleine, head south down Rue Royale, then west along Rue du Faubourg St-Honoré to pass by an A–Z of *haute couture*. On the very first corner (the address is actually 21 Rue Royale) stands Gucci's four floors of marble and mirrors. Further down this same block are Jaeger, Iceberg and the hair stylist Carita, whose clientele includes Catherine Deneuve and Veteran French rocker Johnny Hallyday. Cross the Rue Boissy-d'Anglas and staring you in the face is the Hermès shop, which was opened in 1837 and is now the leading maker of leather goods and scarves (on the top floor is a private museum showing some of the company's historical items, including Napoléon's stirrups, but to visit it you need make arrangements in advance).

If you're a serious style shopper you may never make it to the end of the next block, which has Givenchy, Guy Laroche, Aramis, Ashida, Maxandre and two Yves Saint-Laurent shops, one for clothes and one for his range of beauty products. If you do manage to pass Rue d'Anjou, then keep going and you'll come to Courrèges, Karl Lagerfeld, Cartier, Christian Dior, Pierre Balmain, Lancôme,

Versace, Sonia Rykiel, Ungaro, Pierre Cardin and Christian Lacroix. Those are just some of the names which grace this street, so much so that you may not even notice the American Ambassador's Residence at number 41, the British Embassy at number 39 or the Japanese Embassy at number 31. All three buildings are of great historical interest. The first is rented by the American government from the Rothschild family, the second dates back to 1723 and was bought from Napoléon's sister Pauline by George III in 1815 after the Battle of Waterloo, and the Japanese Embassy was built in 1718.

Route to the guillotine

Also of historical interest is the eastern continuation of Rue du Faubourg St-Honoré, the **Rue St-Honoré**. This runs as far as the Palais Royal near the Louvre and can be traced back to the 12th century, making it one of the oldest streets in central Paris. At number 263 is the church of **Notre-Dame-de-l'Assomption**, which was built in 1676 when it formed part of a convent, while at 269 is the **Église St-Roch**, which was begun even earlier, in 1653, but not completed for another 100 years. Bullet holes in the church have been there since 5 October 1795, when Royalist troops based in the church were fired on, and killed, by an anti-Royalist group led by an unknown soldier named Napoléon Bonaparte. Almost exactly two years earlier, on 6 October 1793, Marie Antoinette had passed down this same street on her way to the guillotine.

115

Place de la Madeleine

*The Église Ste-Marie Madeleine (Church of St Mary Magdalene), known as **La Madeleine**, dominates this square in one of Paris's most refined quarters, and its main financial district. It is a strange building and had a lengthy gestation period. Building began in 1764, but when a new architect took over the job he ripped down what had been put up and began work on a replacement that was modelled on the Panthéon (see pages 62–63).*

> *" Few cities lend themselves so effortlessly to popular expectations as Paris; Paris can deliver what the tourists want without taking on the character of a theme park, and with its dignity unimpaired. But the Parisians are a bloody-minded lot… "*
>
> **Peter Lennon, *Foreign Correspondent* (Picador, 1994)**

Later Napoléon announced that the site should contain a temple dedicated to his Great Army, so yet again the part-built edifice was torn down and restarted. In 1814 Louis XVIII said that the building should be a church and not a temple, and it was eventually consecrated in 1842 – though not until after it had been considered as a possibility for Paris's first railway station!

Music and monuments

The building also has contrasting musical connections. Saint-Saëns became the church organist in 1858, and composed some of his works in the church, while in 1975 the cabaret artist Josephine Baker's funeral service was held at the church, where she was the first American woman to be honoured with a 21-gun salute – quite an honour for someone who had worked at the Folies-Bergère.

The church is surrounded by 52 Corinthian columns, each of them 20m (66ft) high, and the front is approached by a steep flight of 28 steps, at the top of which is a view back down

Rue Royale to the Place de la Concorde and across the Seine to the Hôtel des Invalides with its own golden-domed church. Above the entrance is one of the largest pediment sculptures in the world: *The Last Judgement* by Lemaire. Inside, La Madeleine is full of marble, gilt and dark wood, with a monumental statue behind the high altar depicting Mary Magdalene ascending to heaven.

Paradise for food-lovers

Food lovers wandering round this square will think they too have ascended to foodie heaven, as it has some of the **best food shops in Paris**. Everyone in the city has heard of Fauchon at number 26 (*tel: 47 42 60 11*), even if they can't afford to shop there. Its window displays are a work of art, and enough to make your mouth water and have you reaching for your camera. The shop stocks the very finest produce from all over the world, and claims to have over 20,000 items, including Scottish salmon, Caribbean fruit, a separate Italian delicatessen, a wine cellar and of course the best French produce from the regions. A separate shop contains an even more tempting collection of cakes, pastries and chocolates, and you can try sampling the quality without quite breaking the bank by dining in their own restaurant, with its view of La Madeleine.

Other high-class food shops on the Place include the Boutique Maille at number 6 (*tel: 40 15 06 00*), which specialises in mustard and storage jars, and Hédiard at number 21 (*tel: 43 12 88 88*), an *épicerie* that has been here since 1854 and which rivals Fauchon in its stock of world-wide exotic produce as well as fine French wines. It also has its own restaurant. Just off the square at 4 Boulevard Malesherbes is Au Verger de la Madeleine (*tel: 42 65 51 99*), another long-established family-run *épicerie*, not quite as vast as the others and with more concentration on fine French food and wine.

Place Vendôme

There is a long history behind the turning of **Place Vendôme** into one of the most elegant squares – and addresses – in Paris, where the Ritz Hotel is only one of the many high-class establishments. In 1685 a mansion belonging to the Duke of Vendôme and a Capuchin convent nearby were bought with a view to developing a square which would house important public buildings such as the National Library, the Mint and various Academies, all overlooking a large open space, in the centre of which would be an imposing statue of King Louis XIV.

The façades of houses were erected to create the right impression, but it was not until the early 18th century that various plots of land around the square were bought and the façades were slowly turned into the graceful buildings planned. These still survive to provide a magnificent grand location.

The Austerlitz Column

The king's statue, however, did not survive the Revolution and at the centre of the Place today is a 44m (132ft) high column topped with a statue of Napoléon dressed as Julius Ceasar. The **Austerlitz Column** has a stone core but is surrounded by a

spiral of bronze, cast from over 1200 cannons that Napoléon had captured at the Battle of Austerlitz in 1805 and melted down. The statue and column have also had a chequered history during the turbulent years since the Revolution. In 1814 the statue of Napoléon was replaced by one of Henri IV, which lasted 100 days and was itself replaced by a fleur-de-lis flag. King Louis-Philippe later reinstated Napoléon but in his military costume, and later still Napoléon III erected a copy of the original Caesar-like statue. Column and statue were torn down by the Commune in 1871, supposedly at the instigation of the artist Courbet, who made it look like a pile of manure. For this act he was later exiled and his paintings sold to cover the cost of rebuilding.

Putting on the Ritz

The Place Vendôme continues to have a place in history, as it was from the **Hôtel Ritz** in August 1997 that the late Princess of Wales and Dodi Al-Fayed set out on their final ill-fated car journey. Inside the Ritz is the Hemingway Bar (*entrance off Rue Cambon*), named for the American author who was said to be the first in there for a drink to celebrate the liberation of Paris in 1944. Winston Churchill and Douglas Fairbanks have also raised their glasses here.

Around the square are several extremely expensive jewellers, including Cartier, Boucheron, Van Cleef and Arpels, Piaget and Mikimoto. In one corner is a large branch of Emporio Armani, in the former Hôtel du Rhin, where Napoléon III lived for a while in 1848. Even the anonymous but stylish office buildings have their historical connections, of one kind or another. At number 12 Chopin died in 1849, while at number 16 Franz Anton Mesmer, the Austrian doctor who introduced hypnosis to the world (though he believed it to be some form of magnetism), used to hold meetings to demonstrate his techniques before he became discredited. It was also in this same building that the Obelisk Press, the firm most noted – or notorious – for first publishing Henry Miller's *Tropic of Cancer*, had its offices.

119

> *" In other countries people say things like 'you're looking well', or 'caught a bit of the sun, did you?' to people just back from holiday.' Here in Paris they berate them publicly for scruffiness. "*
>
> **Kate Muir's Diary, *The Times Magazine*, 12 Sept 1998**

Palais Royal

The **Palais Royal** (Royal Palace) was first commissioned in 1632 by the then Prime Minister Cardinal Richelieu, the effective ruler of France at the time. In 1642 Richelieu on his deathbed bequeathed the Palace to Louis XIII. When Louis died the following year, his widow, Anne of Austria, moved from the Louvre and it was only then that the Cardinal's Palace became the Royal Palace. It has been through various hands since, all adding to the history of the buildings and their rather haphazard expansion.

It was Louis-Philippe, Duke of Orléans, who redeveloped the site to raise some much-needed money, and built rows of shops and offices around three sides of the Palace gardens. His idea had been to design a square to rival San Marco in

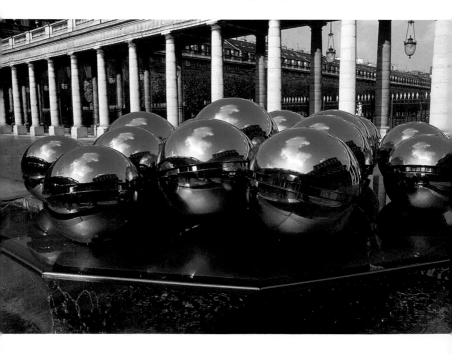

Venice, but the result was much more squalid. The area quickly degenerated because Louis was so desperately in need of money that he rented properties out to anyone, including brothels, gamblers, billiard halls, a wax museum and side-shows. Soon afterwards the Théâtre-Français (now the Comédie-Française) was added in one corner, adding to the jumble of buildings. It was in the gardens that the seeds for the French Revolution are said to have been sewn, and on 13 July 1789 Camille Desmoulins, the Revolutionary leader, here called upon his fellow citizens to take up arms.

From gambling to high culture

The gambling houses were closed down in 1828, and in 1848 the Palace was ransacked by the Paris Commune, who burned much of the historical contents in a giant bonfire. The buildings were then restored in the 1870s. Today they house the Ministry of Culture and some private residences, though the gardens are open to visitors and contain some modern sculptures. One of those in the main courtyard is by Daniel Buren and consists of 280 black-and-white columns of varying heights, with reflective pools and lights. It is yet another example of controversial Parisian development – so much so that the people who still live in the apartments petitioned to have it halted in 1986, but though initially successful this was only a temporary reprieve.

The one-time gambling dens, brothels and billiard halls now contain trade of a rather more refined kind, the pleasant arcades having cafés, bookshops, stamp shops, milliners, furniture makers and other retailers. There are still some private apartments, and past residents have included the writers Cocteau and Colette, the latter having lived at 9 Rue de Beaujolais.

" *I love Paris in the springtime.* **"**
Cole Porter, 'I Love Paris' from
Can-Can

Antiques galore

Between the Palais and the Louvre is what was the Grand Hôtel du Louvre, now **Le Louvre des Antiquaires**. Inside, over 240 antique shops are spread throughout three floors – a real treasure trove, if not necessarily a source of great bargains. There are shops specialising in prints, books, glass, clothes, dolls and documents, as well as general dealers.

Place de l'Opéra

*Seven streets come thundering in to the **Place de l'Opéra**, bringing masses of traffic with them, which was partly Baron Haussmann's plan (give or take a little traffic!) when he redesigned Paris in the late 19th century. The Place then was to be the setting not only for the Paris Opera but also, in Haussmann's grand vision, for a circus around which all this activity would be generated. Today the main activities of the circus are shopping and theatre, dominated and presided over by the Opera House.*

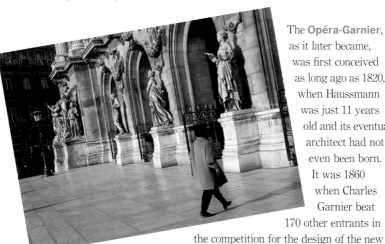

The **Opéra-Garnier**, as it later became, was first conceived as long ago as 1820, when Haussmann was just 11 years old and its eventual architect had not even been born. It was 1860 when Charles Garnier beat 170 other entrants in the competition for the design of the new Opera House. One of his early problems was how to cope with flooding from an underground spring, which he did by transforming it into an artificial lake from which the Paris fire brigade still draws water, and above which were the cellars where lurked the Phantom of the Opera.

When the theatre finally opened in 1875 it was the biggest in the world, covering an area of almost three acres and with a stage large enough to hold 450 people. The astonishing design (and love it or hate it, you can't ignore it) was the architect's reaction against Classical architecture and an attempt to produce a 'Napoléon III' style. It didn't exactly catch on,

> *After five days, I decided to stay in Paris, possibly for ever. I set myself two goals: to fall in love (preferably in the spring), and to become a famous writer (preferably by summer).* **99**

Barry Pilton, *An Innocent Abroad: The Paris Years* (Corgi, 1997)

though if the Opéra-Garnier happens to be open it is worth looking inside to see Garnier's grand foyer and staircase, with their dazzling display of gilt, mirrors, mosaics and paintings. If you do want a night at the opera, you will need to go to the new Opéra-Bastille (*see page 90*), as the Opéra-Garnier is now a showcase for modern dance and classical ballet.

Café to the stars

Across from the Opéra-Garnier is another institution: the **Café de la Paix**. While it might seem an exaggeration to put a café on a par with an opera house, the interior of this one was also designed by Charles Garnier and it is officially classed as a historic landmark. When Hemingway headed for the Ritz to have a drink to celebrate the liberation of Paris on 25 August 1944, General de Gaulle's idea of a celebration was a takeaway from the Café de la Paix. Other famous patrons have included Oscar Wilde, Salvador Dali and Maria Callas. And it is cheaper than a night at the opera – just!

Opposite the Opéra-Garnier is the grand **Avenue de l'Opéra**, designed by Haussmann and begun in 1854, but not finished until 1878 despite having started from both ends. It is now lined by banks, travel agencies and tourist shops concentrating on clothes and perfumes. Behind the Place de l'Opéra runs the **Boulevard Haussmann**, named after the great 19th-century architect himself, and now lined with department stores and chain stores, like a Parisian Oxford Street.

Eating and drinking

There are some hideously expensive eating places in St-Honoré, but plenty of cheaper options too if you want to come here and see the bright lights at night, or find somewhere to relax between bouts of daytime window shopping. But it is worth splashing out, perhaps at one of the restaurants in the gourmet food shops on Place de la Madeleine.

Cafés and Bars

Harry's Bar

5 Rue Daunou. Tel: 42 61 71 14. £££. The prices are elevated but so is the history of those who have drunk here since it opened in 1911, including Scott Fitzgerald, Gloria Swanson, Jean-Paul Sartre and George Gershwin, who, it is said, dreamed up An American in Paris while drinking here. *1045–0400 daily, food 1200–1500.*

Café de la Paix

12 Boulevard des Capucines. Tel: 40 07 30 20. £££ With a sumptuous interior by the man who designed the Paris Opera opposite, you are paying here for the *ambiance* and atmosphere of a place which has attracted the likes of Maurice Chevalier and President Truman. Coffee, beer, wine, sandwiches and simple (but expensive) meals. *1000–0130 daily, food 1200–0100.*

Café Madeleine

1 Rue Tronchet. Tel: 42 65 21 91. ££. A good place to watch the goings-on around the Place, and cheaper than the food stores, cafés and restaurants, if you just want a quick drink. *0730–2100 daily, food all day.*

Ma Bourgogne

133 Boulevard Haussmann. Tel: 45 63 50 61. ££. Excellent award-winning wine bar where you can relax with a glass from a wide and affordable selection, or have a plate of simple but good dishes such as steak, *coq au vin* or the house speciality, *oeufs en Meurette* (which is basically eggs and bacon cooked in red wine). *0700–2200 Mon–Fri, hot food 1200–1430 and 1900–2200.*

Le Val d'Or

28 Avenue Franklin-Roosevelt. Tel: 43 59 95 81. ££. Wine bar with an excellent range, especially from the owner's home region of the Auvergne, which also influences the food: hearty rural cooking. You can also snack on *charcuterie* or quiche, if you wish. Wine has to be bought by the bottle, but you only pay for what you drink. *0800–2100 Mon/Wed/Fri, 0800–2230 Thur.*

" *For me, elegance is not to pass unnoticed but to get to the very soul of what one is.* "

Christian Lacroix, *International Herald Tribune* (Paris 21 Jan 1992)

Restaurants

Fauchon

26 Place de la Madeleine. Tel: 47 42 60 11. ££. With the shop's reputation for fine food, this upstairs restaurant has to maintain its high reputation, and it isn't as expensive or as formal as you might expect. Imaginative dishes, like melon and Sauternes soup. *Lunch and dinner, Mon–Sat.*

Lucas Carton

9 Place de la Madeleine. Tel: 42 65 22 90. £££. Serious food at serious prices from top chef Alain Senderens, though lunch is cheaper. The Art Nouveau décor goes with the *nouvelle cuisine* dishes, such as a signature dish of honey-roasted duck *à l'Apicius* or ravioli filled with clams. *1200–1430 Mon–Fri and 2000–2230 Mon–Sat, closed Aug.*

Le Bristol

Hôtel Bristol, 112 Rue du Faubourg-St-Honoré. Tel: 53 43 43 00. £££. If you want to indulge and hang the expense, this Michel-starred place is as good a choice as any, but don't expect much change out of 1000F. Complex dishes like roast turbot with grilled chestnuts and puréed butternut squash, or truffle and parmesan risotto, make it a price worth paying for serious foodies. *1200–1415 and 1930–2230 daily.*

Shopping

Galeries Lafayette

40 Boulevard Haussmann. Tel: 42 82 34 56. Vast department store for which you really need a map and compass to negotiate your way around. More high street than *haute couture.*

La Maison du Miel

24 Rue Vignon. Tel: 47 42 26 70. The House of Honey has been run by the same family for over 90 years, and the name says it all: dozens of delicious-sounding flavours, along with honey-based products such as soap and wax.

Flower and plant market

Place de la Madeleine. 0800–1930 Tue–Sun.

Caviar Kaspia

17 Place de la Madeleine. Tel: 42 65 33 52. An upmarket version of the shops you often see at airports, selling caviar, smoked salmon and other culinary treats. *0900–0100 Mon–Sat.*

Hédiard

21 Place de la Madeleine. The main rival to Fauchon as the best food store on the block, this place has the best regional produce from France and the best fruit and vegetables from around the world. If it's in season, it's in here, and go even if you only go to look. *Tel: 43 12 88 88. 0940–1900 Mon–Sat.*

La Maison de la Truffe

19 Place de la Madeleine. Tel: 42 65 53 22. The best truffles in season, and when they're not there are plenty of truffle-based products such as oils and vinegars. A unique shop – with a small restaurant attached (and guess what they serve!). *0900–2100 Tue–Sat, 0900–2000 Mon.*

Paris fashions

Paris is still 'where it's at' in the fashion world. Italy may produce the ultimate smooth lines of Armani and Versace, Britain may throw up mavericks like Vivienne Westwood and Alexander McQueen, and the Japanese provide Issey Miyake and Kenzo, but only Paris consistently produces both the chic of Dior and the radical Jean-Paul Gaultier. And Paris is the only city in the world where you can walk into shops and buy clothes by all those designers and more – and sometimes at discount prices.

The designer names all have their showcase outlets, and if you take a stroll down Avenue Montaigne off the Champs-Élysées (*see page 155*) and along Rue du Faubourg St-Honoré (*see page 114*), then you'll have found most of them. But other stores are scattered around the city – Gaultier recently opened one in the newly fashionable Bastille district (*see pages 90–91*), and there are places where you can find designer names at discount prices, and shops which specialise in second-hand gear – with the right label.

ST-HONORÉ

Second-hand chic

Alternatives (*18 Rue du Roi-de-Sicile, Paris 75004; tel: 42 78 31 50*) sells only the best-quality second-hand clothes by the best designers, ranging from Gaultier to Hermès, so prices aren't cheap, but a lot cheaper than buying new. At **L'Habilleur** (*44 Rue de Poitou, Paris 75003; tel: 48 87 77 12*) you can buy ex-catwalk clothes and end-of-line stock, which are acquired direct from the designers. If your tastes run to Dior, Chanel and Prada, the main shop which stocks the best of them second-hand is **Réciproque** (*123 Rue de la Pompe, Paris 75016; tel: 47 04 82 24/47 04 30 28*), which has two shops side-by-side. If you know your clothes and don't mind not having the label to flaunt, designers offload some of their items, labels removed, to **Le Mouton à Cinq Pattes** (*19 Rue Grégoire de Tours, Paris 75006; tel: 43 29 73 56*).

Guided tours

If you need advice, walking tours for fashion shoppers are available from **Promenades de Style** (*52 Rue du Faubourg Poissonière, Paris 75010; tel: 47 70 08 28*). Finally, even if you can't afford any of this gear, you might still be more fashionable than you think. 'Brit chic' is in. There are British designers at Givenchy (Alexander McQueen), Chloe (Stella McCartney) and even Dior (John Galliano). Even Marks and Spencer is fashionable in Paris, so all is not lost.

Montmartre

The touristification of Montmartre, with dozens of artists touting to paint every visitor's portrait – and dozens of tourists to every artist – shouldn't overshadow its racy and cultural past. The ghosts of artists such as Picasso, Dali and Utrillo still haunt its streets and houses, while down the hill in the Pigalle area are the streetwalkers who show that the sex industry is still alive and flourishing. This is the sweaty side of Paris that made it not so much the city of light as the city of sin. Ironically the name Montmartre derives in part from the Mount of the Martyrs, as it was here that three local martyrs were beheaded in the 3rd century AD, though in Roman times it was already the site of a temple dedicated to Mars.

129

Montmartre

Getting there: **Métro:** *Anvers for the funicular up to Sacré-Coeur, Pigalle for Place Pigalle, Blanche for the cemetery or Lamarck-Caulaincourt to start near the top.* **Funicular:** *runs from Place Suzanne Valadon up to Place du Parvis-du-Sacré-Coeur all day, every day, the cost being one Métro ticket.* **Buses:** *30, 54, 68, 74, 80, 81, 85, 95.*

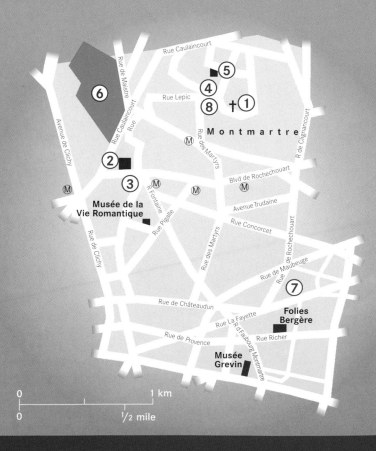

① Sacré-Coeur

This is the sacred amongst all that is profane in Montmartre. The Cathedral of the Sacred Heart looks in some lights like the decoration on top of a wedding cake, but as with a cake there are goodies hidden inside. **Pages 132–133**

② Moulin Rouge

Red Windmill sounds an unlikely name for a sexy cabaret, but this is where the modern striptease was born, where can-can dancers kicked up their legs, and where the tradition of erotic dancing continues, albeit thanks to coach parties of well-heeled visitors. **Page 137**

③ Musée de l'Érotisme

This museum of erotic art continues the Montmartre tradition of pushing back the boundaries by being the first such museum in the city. It houses a world-wide collection on the theme of, well, what makes the world go round. **Page 134**

④ Espace Montmartre Salvador Dali

Not a museum on the Picasso or Rodin scale but a beautiful display of a large range of the artist's work, with a chance to buy some for yourself. **Page 135**

⑤ Montmartre Museum

Only a small collection in what was at one time a country house, but it does give a good broader picture of the story of the area. **Page 135**

⑥ Montmartre Cemetery

The graves here show the glittering history of Montmartre, with Degas, Berlioz and Nijinsky, to name but a few. **Page 134**

⑦ Pigalle at night

You might find it salacious, shocking, titillating, exciting or degrading – or a combination of all those things – but this is Parisian nightlife all-too-literally in the raw. **Pages 136–137, 140–141**

⑧ Place du Tertre

Touristy or not, this is the Montmartre that visitors expect to see: a square bustling with cafés and with people, especially the artists with their easels doing lightning sketches. Just don't expect to be flattered. **Pages 135 and 139**

> " Salvador Dali must've come twenty times. He used to say, 'The Crazy Horse girls are all virgins.' One evening, he arrived and Andy Warhol was here. Dali said, 'Tonight the omens are not good.' He turned on his cane and left. Elvis came one night, brought by a mutual friend. He said, 'I'll come only if you give me a girl for the night.' So the friend had to loan Elvis his fiancée. "

Anthony Weller, 'Les Girls', quoting from Alain Bernardin, founder of the Crazy Horse

Sacré-Coeur ✓

This basilica, begun in 1876, is one of the handful of images that say 'Paris', ranking with the Eiffel Tower, Notre-Dame, the Arc de Triomphe and nowadays the pyramid outside the Louvre. Anything further removed from the graceful simplicity of that pyramid it would be

hard to imagine. Sacré-Coeur looks like a jigsaw puzzle of a church that hasn't been quite put together properly.

The building owes its origins to the disastrous Franco-Prussian War of 1870, when some 58,000 citizens lost their lives. Afterwards a group of Catholics determined to create a church to the Sacred Heart on the hill of Montmartre – the highest point in Paris – as a memorial to the dead. The French state stepped in to help in 1873, and building began three years later using designs drawn up by Paul Abadie. When Abadie himself died in 1884, eight years after construction began, only the foundations were in place. This was due to the fact that the hill was on the site of an old quarry and pylons needed to be sunk to stabilise the building work.

The church was completed in 1914 and the total cost had been 40 million francs. The bell tower which dominates the domes was put up in 1904 and stands some 80m (262ft) high. If you want a spectacular view, however, you must make your way to the top of the church's dome, where you can both look down on the interior of the church and, from an external gallery, look over the Paris skyline for several miles. The gallery is almost at the same height as the Eiffel Tower.

The church interior is not especially noteworthy, though it does have some interesting mosaics and modern stained glass (the original glass was destroyed in 1944). The church also has one of the heaviest bells in the world, weighing in at some 19.5 tons. The church steps are favourite posing places for photos, while yet more exposures are made in the gardens below, which offer great views of the Paris skyline.

The artists' quarter

Several places around Sacré-Coeur are named after artists from the area, such as Rue Maurice Utrillo to the east and Place Suzanne Valadon (Utrillo's daughter, also an artist) at the foot of the funicular. The most amusing name, though, is the square below the church, which is named after a local artist called Willette, who distinguished himself by calling out 'Long live the devil!' when the church was inaugurated. The name was given by opponents to the building of the church, who by the time it was completed were in power.

> " Everything in this city has a quality that defies analysis but enables you to say without any hesitation: 'That is Paris' – even if it is only a milk can dangling from a door knob, or one of those coarse brooms sweeping up the leaves at the pavement's edge in October with a sound like the sea, or an array of tired-looking volumes in a bookseller's box on the embankment between the pont Neuf and the pont Royal. "
>
> **Julian Green, *Paris*, translated by J A Underwood**

Sacré-Coeur is not the only church here. Take a look at the **Église St-Pierre**, just across the street to the west, and thought by some to be the oldest church in Paris. Although that claim is disputed, it is certainly among the oldest two or three, dating back to the early 12th century, a few years earlier even than the grand Notre-Dame.

133

Montmartre museums and cemeteries

Montmartre has always been a district in which life has been lived to the full – sometimes short-lived at that. A stroll around its cemeteries and museums shows not only some of the very distinguished names associated with the place, but also the way in which they lived their lives – bursting with artistic or sexual expression, and frequently both.

Erotic Museum

Take the Métro to Blanche and a short way east is the unmissable façade of the **Musée de l'Érotisme**. The huge yet discreet back view of a nude woman leaves no illusions as to what is beyond its doors. It is in fact a serious look at the ways in which arts and crafts worldwide, from the ancient to the challengingly modern, have dealt with the erotic. There are African masks adorned with copulating couples, Japanese sex manuals, and Indonesian drums in the form of men with phalluses so large you could play baseball with them. An incredible seven floors is divided up into permanent exhibitions, with over 1500 items, and changing contemporary exhibitions of paintings, photography and ceramics. For those looking for extremely unusual presents, there is also a gift shop.

Montmartre Cemetery

Back past the Blanche Métro and the Moulin Rouge on the right is the **Cimetière de Montmartre**. This densely-packed graveyard has a map near the entrance in case you wish to pay homage to some of the great people buried here, such as Degas, Berlioz, Dumas, Offenbach, Nijinsky, Stendhal, the cabaret dancer 'La Goulou' and film director François Truffaut. You would be advised to memorise or copy the map, as the cemetery is quite large and some of the graves can be hard to find.

Return to the entrance and take Rue Caulaincourt, which is a slower and gentler climb up to Montmartre than the challenge of the Sacré-Coeur steps. Once the road has turned to the right, and eventually started to level out, you will see up a side road on the right the entrance to another cemetery, that of St-Vincent – more modest, but memorably situated with a view up to Sacré-Coeur. Among those resting here are the composer Honegger and the painter Utrillo.

Montmartre Museum

To learn more about Utrillo's association with Montmartre, continue along Rue Caulaincourt and take the first right past the cemetery, following the signs for the **Musée de Montmartre**. On the way you will pass the celebrated cabaret Au Lapin Agile and the Montmartre vineyards. The Montmartre Museum is entered through the house in which Utrillo, Renoir, Dufy and Suzanne Valadon once lived, and though the disparate collection of paintings, ceramics, documents and photographs may not detain you for long, they nevertheless give some good historical background to the area you are now in.

Place du Tertre

Before making your way to the Sacré-Coeur itself, head for **Place du Tertre**, around the corner from which is the **Espace Montmartre Salvador Dali**. This impressive basement gallery, in which new rooms seem to continue to appear as you wander round, contains a large collection of the Spanish artist's sculptors, paintings, prints and engravings – not to mention some amusing photographs of the famous moustache. You can even treat yourself to a signed print, with prices starting from a reasonable few thousand francs but soaring dramatically upwards.

In the nearby cemetery of the **Église St-Pierre** (*see page 133*) there are few of the famous names which distinguish the larger Montmartre Cemetery, but one notable grave is the man who gave his name to the area at the foot of Montmartre hill, the sculptor Jean-Baptiste Pigalle (1714–85).

Pigalle

Although most visitors to Paris take in Montmartre, far fewer bother with Pigalle at the foot of the hill. Most of those that go there know full well its reputation as the Soho of Paris, and go for that reason. But to call it Soho is to play down the much raunchier approach to sex that the Parisians have. Live sex shows are advertised openly – though the French call it 'Life Sex' – and as in all such areas in the world, you have to take care: what you are promised and what you get may be very different, both in terms of what's on stage and the cost of seeing it (and the accompanying drinks). If you are easily offended, the area around Place Pigalle is not somewhere to take a night-time stroll, as the photographs and rubber dolls on display leave nothing to the imagination.

This is the world of Henry Miller, of *Tropic of Cancer* and *Quiet Days in Clichy*, with Place Clichy at the western end of Boulevard de Clichy, on which Place Pigalle stands. The boulevard's continuation, Boulevard de Rochechouart, is the other sleazy street, although most of the action – and promises of action – take place on Clichy in the short stretch between the Pigalle and Blanche Métro stations. Most city coach tours that take visitors to Montmartre will pass by here and give passengers a teasing glimpse of naughty Paris, as they pass by the Moulin Rouge.

The Moulin Rouge

The **Moulin Rouge** today is the respectable side of the sex industry, and gives visitors a slightly raunchier version of its famed 19th-century showgirl and can-can shows, so vividly painted by Toulouse-Lautrec. Who would have thought that his paintings of a risqué cabaret would end up on the walls of one of the city's greatest art museums, the Musée d'Orsay? His renowned posters are probably even more widely used today to publicise the shows than they were at the time, while some of his pastels in the Musée capture the pathos and mundane reality behind the glamorous façade.

" *To see a performance makes one wonder, naturally and perversely, what these girls look like with their clothes on. Albert Camus spoke for many of us when he said, 'It hurts me to confess it, but I would gladly trade ten conversations with Einstein for one first encounter with a pretty chorus girl.'* "

Anthony Weller, 'Les Girls'

Showgirls and cabaret

Pigalle is not just about sex, though it is very much about nightlife. During the day its streets can have a ghost-town atmosphere, broken only by the sight of a 'good-time girl' leaning in a doorway or alleyway. As darkness falls and the neon turns on, the area is transformed like a woman who layers on the make-up. While tourists flock to the Moulin Rouge, Parisians go to the **Folies Pigalle**, whose cabaret has become a fashionable night out. The spirit of cabaret still lives on here, and up the hill in Montmartre, the **Lapin Agile** cabaret is as popular now as it ever was. Cabaret is used in the traditional sense, incorporating not just showgirls but singers, comedians, speciality acts and even satirical poetry. Of course you don't need to be able to speak French to appreciate a showgirl.

137

Eating and drinking

Take care in Montmartre, as in any area popular with tourists, because there are plenty of places waiting to part you from your francs without providing good quality in return, as they know they'll never see you again. If a place is filled with large coach parties of overseas visitors, be wary: they probably offer a good deal to the tour company. If, however, a place is buzzing with local people who are quite clearly at home there, you are probably safe.

Cafés and Bars

La Fourni

74 Rue des Martyrs. Tel: 42 64 70 35. *££*. Fashionable Pigalle bar attracting wealthy and hip Parisian youth as well as tourists who wander in from the surrounding streets of sleaze. Small range of easy eats like 'le sandwich', larger range of pricey coffees, beers and wines. *0830–0200 Mon–Sat, 1030–0200 Sun, food daily 1100–2300.*

No Problemo

14 Rue Charles-Nodier. Tel: 42 54 39 38. ££. Quirky bar off the tourist track just to the east of the gardens below Sacré-Coeur – so ideal for a pick-me-up or a bit of fortification for the Alpine streets of Montmartre. Serves beer, coffee, wine and a range of bar snacks. *1800–0200 daily.*

Le Progrès

1 Rue Yvonne-le-Tac. Tel: 42 51 33 33. £. Neighbourhood café/bar in the streets between Pigalle and Sacré-Coeur, with a great view of the dome. Cheap but decent grub, and a popular hang-out for young locals. Snacks served all day. *1000–0200 Mon–Sat, lunch 1200–1500.*

Restaurants

Beauvilliers

52 Rue Lamarck. Tel: 42 54 54 42. £££. The best and most expensive restaurant in the area, popular with visiting stars and politicians. A testimony to the food is that Paul Bocuse, probably France's most revered chef, dines here when in Paris. Exquisite inventive cooking but an informal atmosphere for such *haute cuisine*. *1200–1400 and 1930–2230 Tue–Sat, 1930–2230 Mon.*

Le Moulin à Vins

6 Rue Burq. Tel: 42 52 81 27, ££. Wholesome country cooking from the French regions attracts lots of local people to this unpretentious little back-street place, which also has a popular wine bar at the front. Excellent wine list and good value, but book first and come with a healthy appetite. *1800–2400 Tue–Sat, also 1200–1500 Wed–Thur. Closed Aug.*

La Table d'Anvers

2 Place d'Anvers. Tel: 48 78 35 21. £££. Just off the brash Boulevard de Rochechouart is this gastronomic retreat, which offers the best of formal French cuisine with some Italian influences and calorie-packed puddings. *1200–1430 and 1900–2330 Mon–Sat.*

Clubs and nightlife

See also the feature on **Naked Paris** *on pages 140–141.*

La Cigale

120 Boulevard de Rochechouart. Tel: 42 23 15 15. Entrance fee. A well-established disco club in a former theatre. Tends to move with the musical times and also covers a wide range of musical tastes. *2030–0600 daily.*

Le Divan du Monde

75 Rue des Martyrs. Tel: 44 92 77 66. Entrance fee. Live music early evening, later raving to DJs till dawn, this is an eclectic place, with rock, reggae, acid, Latin American, gay and other sessions. *1930–0600 daily.*

Folies Pigalle

11 Place Pigalle. Tel: 40 36 71 58. Entrance fee. Despite the name and location, this isn't a showgirl cabaret but a fashionable disco club with music from rock to rap. Popular with gays and outrageous dressers. *2300–0700 Thur–Sat, 1500–2000 Sun.*

Le Locomotive

90 Boulevard de Clichy. Tel: 53 41 88 88. Entrance fee. This is where the teenagers go while the tourists are packing the Moulin Rouge next door. With three floors all featuring different music, and different theme nights, it's important to check what's on in a local entertainment guide like *Pariscope*. *2300–0600 daily.*

" *Liberté! Fraternité! Sexualité!* "

Graffito in the Paris Métro, 1980s

Shopping

Place du Tertre is the place to buy art works whose paint is still drying, and indeed to buy a portrait of yourself. Try haggling if it's not too busy, but there are few times of year when this square is really quiet. Don't miss the gift shop close by in the Espace Montmartre Salvador Dali: even if you can't afford a limited-edition print, you can buy Dali ties, watches and other unusual items.

Even more unusual souvenirs can be bought in the sex shops around Pigalle, of course, but if you want something erotic rather than pornographic, then try the shop at the Musée de l'Érotisme. For a permanent souvenir by way of a tattoo, visit one of Paris's best tattoo artists (everything is an art in Paris!): Bruno, in his parlour at 4 Rue Germain-Pilon.

The Marché St-Pierre to the east of the foot of Sacré-Coeur is a clothes and fabric market on several floors, with everything from cheap socks to Asian silks. *2 Rue Charles-Nodier; tel: 46 06 92 25. 1330–1830 Tue–Sat.*

Naked Paris: red lights and the Moulin Rouge

The Parisian showgirl, typified by the tall and topless Bluebell Girl (who is as likely to be British as French), can be seen every night in the city's cabarets, of which the most famous are: the Moulin Rouge, the Lido, the Crazy Horse and the Folies-Bergère.

High-tech entertainment

Each has its own speciality, the **Moulin Rouge** being home to the can-can, and the **Lido** to the Bluebell Girls, while the **Crazy Horse** takes the 'artistic nudity' approach. **The Lido** prides itself on its state-of-the-art stage shows, laser lighting, revolving stages and the 60-strong troupe of statuesque dancers. It has an 1100-seat theatre, 70 stereo speakers, seven tons of spotlights, a 23,000-litre fountain and 32km of fibre-optic cables, all run by a suite of 12 computers.

MONTMARTRE

If you want to take in dinner and a show, then expect little change from about 750F, and don't expect *haute cuisine*. You can simply sit at the bar and watch the show, which is much cheaper, but the cost of drinks will mount up. You can find out details of the latest shows and prices in *Pariscope*.

There are many other places offering similar entertainment, though their names are less well known around the world. **Brasil Tropical**, **Elephant Bleu**, **American Dream** and **Carrousel de Paris** are just some of the cabaret clubs providing titillating shows that might include belly dancers, conjurers, acrobats, circus acts and even 'The Full Monty' from all-male dance groups.

Pay your money, make your choice

Less public is the steamier side of the sex business, but the pages of *Pariscope* or *Allo Paris* will also cover the clubs where a bare breast would be the very least the customers expected. Clubs with names like **Show Girls**, **Club 183**, and the strange-sounding **Loving Chair–French Lover's Theatre**, all offer erotic entertainment, from the more conventional striptease acts to harder-core performances of 'Life Sex', in heterosexual, gay or lesbian versions. The latest trend is for private shows, where the girl chosen by the customer will give an erotic dance display in a private room – at a price. And these are the shows that advertise, so you can imagine what entertainment might be available in the back-street dives in the streets around the Place Pigalle.

The Right Bank

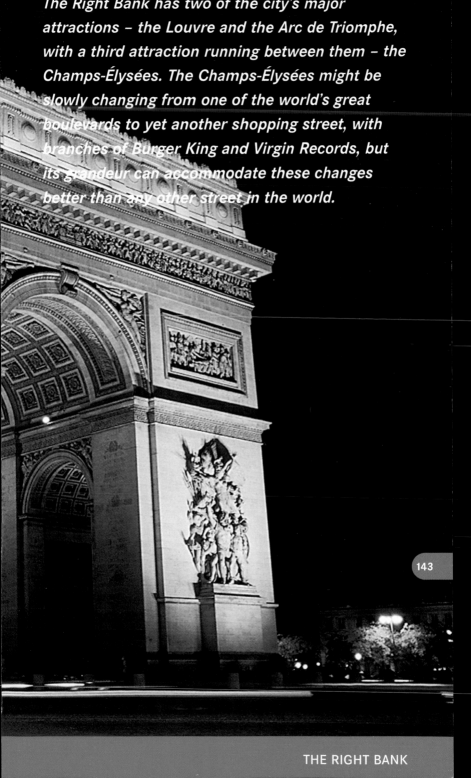

The Right Bank has two of the city's major attractions – the Louvre and the Arc de Triomphe, with a third attraction running between them – the Champs-Élysées. The Champs-Élysées might be slowly changing from one of the world's great boulevards to yet another shopping street, with branches of Burger King and Virgin Records, but its grandeur can accommodate these changes better than any other street in the world.

BEST OF
The Right Bank

Getting there: **Métro:** *Palais Royal–Musée du Louvre for the Louvre; Concorde or Tuileries for the Tuileries; Charles de Gaulle Étoile for Arc de Triomphe/Tourist Office.*
RER: *None in this area.* **Buses:** *Louvre/Tuileries 21, 24, 27, 39, 48, 67, 68, 69, 72, 75, 76, 81, 85, 95; Arc de Triomphe/Tourist Office 2, 30, 31, 52, 73, 92.*

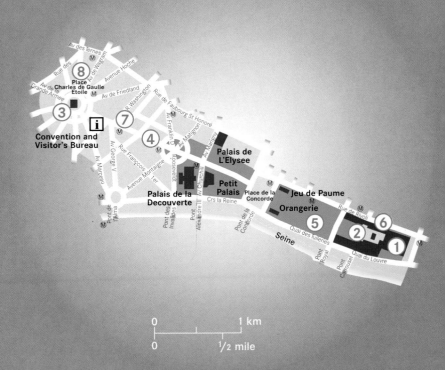

① Visit the world's greatest museum

The biggest collection of arts and artefacts in the world, housed in the biggest building in Paris – and won't you know it after several hours of walking around! The Louvre is an essential visit, though one visit will not be enough to see everything, especially with new wings opening for the Millennium. **Pages 146–149**

② Go back and see it again at night

At night when many of the crowds have gone, and the buildings are floodlit, you can appreciate more the beauty of the Louvre itself. The glass pyramid, lit by a golden light, is also extremely beautiful, as are many of the other buildings around.

③ Climb to the top of the Arc de Triomphe

The majestic arch which stands at the top of the Champs-Élysées can be appreciated from a distance, but the views of the streets around are impressive if you climb up the stairs inside to the top. **Pages 156–157**

④ Stroll along the Champs-Élysées

Paris's high street, one of the most famous street names in the world, may not be quite the grand shopping and strolling experience it once was, but those wide pavements and trees leading up to the Arc de Triomphe at the top are still lovely to see, and you could perhaps risk an over-priced cup of coffee for the pleasure of simply being there. **Pages 152–153**

⑤ Sit in the Jardin des Tuileries

Paris's favourite park, laid out in the 17th century, and still as popular as ever with strollers, lovers, children, tourists and workers with an hour to spare and a need to get away from the traffic. **Pages 150–151**

⑥ See styles past in the Musée de la Mode et du Textile

Paris fashions over the years are on display in this smart, low-light museum, where the clothes are the stars under the spotlight. Admire them all, from wacky to classy, and see how designers have trawled the world for inspiration. **Pages 148–149**

⑦ Have a night out at the Lido

It may be touristy, it may seem old-fashioned, but the multi-million-pound spectacle at the Lido, with its Bluebell Girls, is 'very Paris'. **Page 160**

⑧ Treat yourself to a meal at Guy Savoy

You'll need to book long before you leave home, but Guy Savoy is one of the most highly-rated chefs in Paris, combining the best of traditional cuisine with the adventure of *nouvelle cuisine* in his eponymous restaurant near the Arc de Triomphe. **Page 158**

Tourist information

The city's main tourist office is at the top of the Champs-Élysées, on the south side, and well-stocked with books, leaflets, souvenirs, a currency exchange and knowledgeable staff. *127 Avenue des Champs-Élysées. Tel: 49 52 53 54. 0900–2000 daily.*

The Louvre

*The Louvre is without doubt the greatest art collection
and museum in the world, not only for the size and
scale of the collection, but also the quality. You may
see more Greek statues in Greece, and more Egyptian
remains in Egypt, but the superb examples that are
housed in the Louvre are beyond compare.*

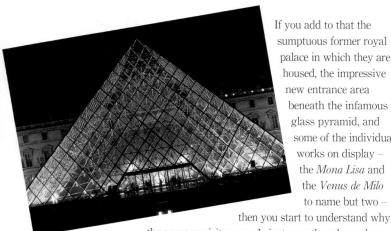

If you add to that the
sumptuous former royal
palace in which they are
housed, the impressive
new entrance area
beneath the infamous
glass pyramid, and
some of the individual
works on display –
the *Mona Lisa* and
the *Venus de Milo*
to name but two –
then you start to understand why
the average visitor spends just over three hours here,
and why such a visit needs to be planned in advance (*open
0900–1800 Thur–Sun, 0900–2145 Mon and Wed*).

Strategies to beat the queues

Arriving about 20 minutes before opening time rather than
mid-morning should save you at least an hour of extra
waiting time. Alternatively, wait until later in the afternoon,
or go to one of the midweek evening openings.

The main entrance is through the glass pyramid, but there
is a less-frequented entrance on Rue de Rivoli, near Rue de
Rohan, and it is also much easier to enter the Louvre by
going into the underground Carrousel du Louvre shopping
complex, which links with the shops and ticket offices of the
Louvre beneath the pyramid. Look for the entrance signs on
Rue de Rivoli and the steps down into the complex in Place
du Carrousel.

Priorities

Having bought your ticket beneath the pyramid and picked up the essential museum map, you are faced with three entrances to the different wings of the Louvre: Denon, Sully and Richelieu. If time is scarce and you want to see the highlights, head for the Denon wing. On the first floor in room number 6 is the tiny *Mona Lisa*, and beyond room number 1, on the large staircase down to the ground floor, is the huge *Winged Victory of Samothrace*. From here, enter the Sully wing and follow the signs for the *Venus de Milo*, stunningly displayed and visible from a distance at the end of a corridor of antiquities. Beyond here are two floors of Egyptian antiquities, of which the Louvre has a breathtaking collection.

The collections

Until you have seen the Louvre's collections, it is hard to appreciate their size and their quality. There are over 200 rooms on three floors in its three wings, with a new wing due to open for the Millennium. It has over 400,000 items, although there is not enough space to display more than a fraction of these at any one time. It includes a collection of European painting from 1400 to 1900, which includes work by Rubens, El Greco, Leonardo da Vinci, Turner, Reynolds, Watteau, Van Dyck, Bosch, Vermeer, Géricault and many, many other great names. European sculpture from 1100 to 1900 is also well represented.

With the collections of antiquities it is hard to know where to begin, or indeed to end. The Egyptian collection is vast and ranges from the hugely impressive – an enormous sphinx, and complete crypts and burial chapels – to the tiny and intimate, such as children's toys or fishermen's nets, which amazingly have survived for thousands of years and bring the people back to life for us again.

147

The Greek sculpture is also impressive, and includes two of the Louvre's most famous acquisitions: the *Venus de Milo* and the *Winged Victory of Samothrace*. Both are from the Hellenistic period (3rd–2nd centuries BC) and both impress in very different ways, the *Venus* for its sensual beauty despite its great familiarity, and the *Winged Victory* for its scale and power.

Around the Louvre ✓

Beyond the eye-catching pyramid, and the balancing inverted pyramid in the Place du Carrousel, stands the ***Arc de Triomphe du Carrousel.*** *This was completed in 1808 to celebrate Napoléon's 1805 military victories at Austerlitz and elsewhere. It was actually begun in 1806, the same year as the Arc de Triomphe, but the larger arch was not completed until 1836.*

This can be seen through the smaller arch, which looks straight through the fountains in the Jardin des Tuileries, across the Obelisk of Luxor in the Place de la Concorde, and along the Champs-Élysées to the Arc de Triomphe some two miles away. Beyond that, a straight line extends to yet another arch, the Grande Arche at La Défense. On top of the Carrousel arch are replicas of the bronze horses from San Marco in Venice, the originals of which Napoléon had captured and placed on his ceremonial arch (these were returned in 1815 and replaced with copies). The name Carrousel comes from a military and theatrical tournament that was held in the square in 1662 to celebrate the birth of the Dauphin (the eldest son of the King).

Museums of advertising and fashion

Look north from here and in the wings of the Louvre which you can see are housed the **Musée des Arts Décoratifs** (Museum of Decorative Arts), the **Musée de la Publicité** (Poster and Advertising Museum) and the **Musée de la Mode et du Textile** (Costume and Fashion Museum). The last of these is by far the most interesting for the average visitor to the city of fashion (*107 Rue de Rivoli; tel: 44 55 57 50; 1100–1800 Tue/Thur–Fri, 1100–2200 Wed, 1000–1800 Sat–Sun*). It is not a vast collection but elegantly displayed on two floors. The theme of the displays changes constantly, but you can expect to see original catwalk clothes by designers such as Galliano, Dior, Christian Lacroix and Alexander McQueen, as well as older examples of Parisian clothes, fabrics and accessories. Some displays trace the influence of, for example, tribal arts or the Far East on fashion design, while others may focus on the development of an individual designer. Rapt fashion students study the displays, sketchbooks in hand.

" *For a fiver or so a cup, Angelina's tearoom serves divine hot chocolate, which is exactly that – a melted-down family-size bar of dark in every cup. Naturally, some are unable to steel themselves against the sugar rush, and it was thus that my French friend found herself flat on her back outside the tearoom on the Rue de Rivoli, being revived by a handsome man who was holding her legs in the air and making the questionable statement: 'Mademoiselle, I'm a doctor.'* "

Kate Muir's Diary, *The Times Magazine*, 12 Sept 1998

The applied arts

The **Musée des Arts Décoratifs** (*107 Rue de Rivoli; tel: 44 55 57 50; 1230–1800 Tue/Thur–Fri, 1000–1800 Wed/Sat–Sun*) has recently been partly renovated, with new displays due to be added in 1999, including a 20th-century gallery. The displays cover sculpture, furnishings, wallpapers, woodwork, paintings and many other decorative items from medieval times up to the more outlandish creations of the present day.

Advertising posters

The **Musée de la Publicité** (*107 Rue de Rivoli; tel: 44 55 58 50; 1230–1800 Tue/Thur–Fri, 1000–1800 Wed/Sat–Sun*) is for those interested in advertising and publicity, its core being a collection of some 40,000 posters from 1700 to the present day, augmented by other forms of advertising and pieces from graphic artists who work in this field.

Jardin des Tuileries

*What might merely seem to the visitor to be a pleasant park in the centre of Paris has greater resonance for the residents who are familiar with its history. The **Jardin des Tuileries** was for a long time nothing more than a rubbish pit, whose clay was dug out and used for the making of tiles – tuiles in French. In 1563 Catherine de Medici, who was Regent of France at the time as her son King Charles IX was still under age, decided that living in the Louvre wasn't enough and she wanted a château built right next to it, on the Tuileries.*

This château never materialised as Catherine was worried by an unfavourable horoscope. Later that century Henri IV continued with the development on the Tuileries, and by 1664 Louis XIV was living in the Tuileries while work was being done on the Louvre. In 1715 Louis XV was permanently installed in the Tuileries, until he moved the court to Versailles in 1722.

In view of such extravagance – amongst many others – it is hardly surprising that in 1792, during the Revolutionary

years, the palace at the Tuileries was invaded and the King seized. A few months later the palace was attacked again and ransacked, with 600 Swiss Guards being killed in the process. The palace once again became a royal residence in the 19th century until it was finally burned down by the Paris Commune in 1871.

Gardens for all

What remains are the gardens, which were first laid out in 1649 for Louis XIV, initially for the use of the Royal Family only, until the public was allowed access in the late 17th century. The gardens were improved in the 18th century and have recently undergone another wave of improvements, so that they remain an attractive place to be, much valued by visitors and local residents alike. Here you will see children running around or playing with their boats in the fountains.

There are quiet places to sit and read the paper, or for old friends to have a gossip. There are some impressive statues by Aristide Maillol (*see page 42*) and others, with cafés and several amusements for children.

> " *I was much taken by a nation whose press would print learned disquisitions on the state of the language. Indeed,* Le Monde's *weekly 'Defence of the French Language' read like a rallying call to arms. Consistently to devote a third of a page to tracing the history of a grammatical felicity or logging the mystery fall from grace of an adjective, was the undeniable hallmark of civilization, and was to become the fount of my lifelong love affair with linguistic pedantry. "*

Barry Pilton, *An Innocent Abroad: The Paris Years* (Corgi, 1997)

For a long time visitors were drawn to the gardens in their millions by the presence, in the northwest corner, of the **Jeu de Paume** gallery. This used to house Paris's impressive collection of Impressionist art, until it became obvious that the building was too small to cope with the crowds that were drawn to it. The collection was transferred to the Musée d'Orsay (*see pages 40–41*), the gallery was spruced up, and it is now used to house changing exhibitions of contemporary art – so check what is on in a publication like *Pariscope*.

The Orangery

You will also need to check the situation at the other gallery in the Tuileries, the **Orangerie** in the southwest corner. This houses the Walter-Guillaume Collection of Impressionist Art, which has some gems, although not on the immense scale of the Musée d'Orsay collection. The star attractions are the vast Monet water-lily canvases, housed in two huge special display rooms on the ground floor, where they fill the walls and make the viewer almost giddy with colour. However, the Orangerie is to be closed from the summer of 1999 until late in 2001 for refurbishment, to bring the rest of the display areas up to the same standard as the impressive Monet rooms.

The Champs-Élysées

*There were once fields here, although certainly not the Elysian Fields that the **Avenue des Champs-Élysées** is named for – a name it acquired in 1709. It was mostly marshland until the late 17th century, when the view from the Jardin des Tuileries was extended along what is now the Champs-Élysées to provide a tree-lined vista. In 1724 it was extended as far as the top of the rise at Étoile, now the site of the Arc de Triomphe (see pages 156– 157), and in 1772 even further to Neuilly, in the far west of the city. Even today the road is virtually straight, right out into the distant suburbs, although only the section as far as the Arc de Triomphe is called the Champs-Élysées.*

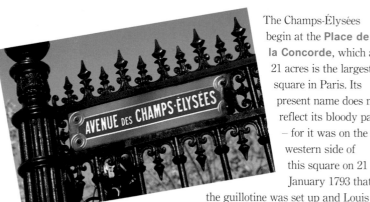

The Champs-Élysées begin at the **Place de la Concorde**, which at 21 acres is the largest square in Paris. Its present name does not reflect its bloody past – for it was on the western side of this square on 21 January 1793 that the guillotine was set up and Louis XVI was beheaded. On 28 July 1794 the square was packed as people clamoured to watch the execution of Robespierre, who had been instrumental in organising the Reign of Terror that brought the downfall of the monarchy, but who had quickly antagonised his fellow-members of the National Convention and had been conspired against and sentenced to death. In all, some 1343 people were executed here in the Place de la Révolution, which was subsequently renamed Concorde: peace.

Egyptian obelisk

In the centre of the square is the **Obelisk of Luxor**, the most ancient monument in Paris – 3300 years old. It weighs in at 220 tons and was a gift in 1831 from the Viceroy of Egypt, Mohammed Ali Pasha, to King Louis-Philippe, who had been crowned the previous year. The 23m (76ft) tall monument was originally in the Temple of Luxor, and was not erected here until 1836. If you can brave the traffic and cross to the centre to take a close look at the obelisk, you will see carvings depicting its journey from Luxor to the French capital, via Alexandria and all the way around the French coast to Normandy.

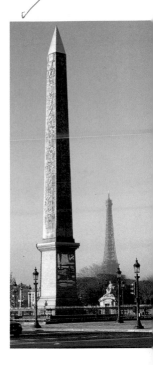

Place of celebration

From the Place de la Concorde, the Avenue leads up past the **Grand Palais** and **Petit Palais** (*see pages 154–155*), past the Rond-Point des Champs-Élysées, and to the stretch which most people think of when you mention the name: the long, wide boulevard with the impressive sight of the **Arc de Triomphe** at the top. This is where Parisians gather at times of national importance, whether it be to celebrate the Liberation of Paris in 1944 or winning the World Cup in 1998. At 71m (233ft) it is the second-widest street in the capital (only the Avenue Foch, which runs southwest from the Arc de Triomphe, is wider). Today it is a busy shopping thoroughfare, lined with banks, airline offices, pavement cafés, fast-food places and car showrooms. There are several shopping arcades, though, running off the street on the northern side, and some of these have rather more upmarket fashion shops. They begin just east of the Rue de Berri, down from the Georges V Métro station.

> " [France] witnessed the first parachute descent, two centuries ago from a balloon above the Parc Monceau in Paris – the intrepid jumper had prudently tried it on his dog beforehand. "
>
> **Jonathan Fenby, *On the Brink* (Little, Brown and Co, 1998)**

153

Around the Champs-Élysées

*Off Place de la Concorde, the Parisian traffic and pedestrians cross the Seine on the **Pont de la Concorde** – a bridge built in 1791, and partly made with stone remnants from the storming of the Bastille so that the people could forever trample on the ruins of the hated old fortress. Head up the Champs-Élysées from Concorde and you will pass between, on your right, the gardens and rear grounds of the Palais de l'Élysée, the Presidential Palace, and, to the left, first the Petit Palais then the Grand Palais.*

The Little Palace

The **Petit Palais** was built for the Universal Exhibition of 1900 (the first world fair to be held in Paris) in order to house a display of French art. Today it is the home of the Fine Arts Museum: the Musée du Petit Palais (*Avenue Winston Churchill; tel: 42 65 12 73; 1000–1745 Tue–Sun*). The central part of the exhibition is the city's own fine arts collection, which includes paintings by Courbet, Ingres and Delacroix alongside Greek sculpture and examples of Paris's sculpted monuments that have been preserved over the years. This collection has been enhanced by bequests, including the Dutuit collection of antiques, paintings, furniture and Renaissance art objects, and the Tuck bequest of 18th-century furniture and *objets d'art*. In addition, the Palais has temporary exhibition space and has some unusual displays here, often of collections that are travelling round the world, so it is well worth checking what is on during your visit.

The Great Palace

Across the Avenue Winston Churchill is the **Grand Palais** (*Avenue Winston Churchill; tel: 44 13 17 17*), also built for the 1900 exhibition, but as its name suggests a grander structure, with an impressive main staircase, a glass roof, Art Nouveau ironwork and huge bronze statues adding to its imposing nature. Whether you will be able to see the interior depends on whether an exhibition is on at the time, as there is no permanent collection on display here and it could be housing anything from a major touring art exhibition to a car show. Ring to check. If the inside is out of bounds, try at least to see the exterior, dramatically illuminated at night.

Stravinsky and Diaghilev

Fashion shoppers must on no account miss a walk down the **Avenue Montaigne**, which runs from the Rond-Point des Champs-Élysées towards the Seine and the Place de l'Alma, near which is the **Théâtre des Champs-Élysées**. This has one of the finest auditoriums in the city, in which Stravinsky first directed his ballet *Rite of Spring* and as a result had to flee from the outraged audience. Diaghilev has danced on this stage, as has Nureyev and a half-naked Josephine Baker. It is to fashion that the Avenue owes its fame, though, and designers from the traditional (Dior) to the outrageous (Westwood) have either their own shops or outlets selling their fashions. **Dior** is at number 30 (*tel: 40 73 54 40*) with a three-storey shop, and other names to look for include **Chanel** at number 42 (*tel: 47 23 74 12*) and **Nina Ricci** at number 39 (*tel: 49 52 56 00*).

" *Paris loves lovers.* "
Cole Porter, 'Silk Stockings'

Arc de Triomphe ②✓

Perhaps Paris's most familiar monument after the Eiffel Tower stands at the top of the Champs-Élysées in the centre of the Place Charles-de-Gaulle. The latter is also known as the Place de l'Étoile, or Star Square, because 12 avenues radiate out from here – hence the Métro station is called Charles-de-Gaulle–Étoile (nothing to do with the star-like qualities of the former French President).

The unique design of the square is why it has been chosen to be transformed for the night of 31 December 1999 into the biggest clock in the world, its 12 avenues turned into illuminated hands to count down the minutes to the next Millennium. A light of a different kind burns here constantly, as beneath the Arch is the **Tomb of the Unknown Soldier** – a French soldier who died during World War I. The eternal flame has burned since it was first lit on 11 November 1923, and the Remembrance Day Service is held here every year on that date.

Napoléon's triumph

Plans for the Arch began in 1806, when Napoléon decided he wanted something quite special in honour of his triumphant military forces. Something special is what he got, as it took two years just to lay the foundations. In 1810 the arch was still nowhere near completion, and the Emperor was due to marry the Hapsburg Archduchess, Marie-Louise, whom he wanted to introduce to Paris in traditional fashion in a procession along the Champs-Élysées. To add to the grandeur a dummy arch of painted canvas was constructed, and the real arch was not in fact completed until 1836. Sadly, only four years later, Napoléon's body was to pass beneath the arch in his funeral procession.

Over the years the Arc de Triomphe has witnessed many other great occasions: state weddings and funerals, the Liberation celebrations in 1944 and, most recently, packed crowds celebrating France's victory over Brazil in the World Cup Finals of 1998, which were held in France.

Battles and generals

The arch impresses from almost any angle, being 50m (164ft) high by 45m (148ft) across. Access is by an underground passage which connects with the Métro station, and is during opening hours only (*1000–2230 daily*). The Arch is worth a close look, to see the amount of detail in the statues and reliefs that cover the structure. These commemorate many events, such as the Battle of Austerlitz and the Battle of Aboukir, while 30 shields near the top bear the names of 30 Napoleonic victories. Stairs inside the arch lead up to a viewing platform from which there is a terrific view straight down the Champs-Élysées, as well as others down the other avenues which spread out from here. In keeping with the spirit of the Arch, several of them such as Avenue Foch (the widest street in Paris) are named after important French military leaders. A night-time trip to the top of the Arc de Triomphe is also highly recommended.

Eating and drinking

There is plenty of choice, as elsewhere in Paris, though you can expect to pay a lot if you want a pavement seat in one of the cafés or bistros lining the Champs-Élysées. It might be worth it, though, just once for the experience. The price here will be a pittance, however, compared to your bill should you choose to splash out and eat at one of the city's best restaurants, Guy Savoy (see below). There are plenty of other good but less bank-breaking choices too.

Cafés and Bars

Barfly

49–51 Avenue George-V. Tel: 53 67 84 60. £££. Absolutely *the* place for the beautiful people to see and be seen, though if you're dressed smartly enough you can get past the doormen and at least have a drink at the bar to do some celeb-spotting. Food is served too in the restaurant – a mix of sushi (or whatever else becomes fashionable) and standard French cuisine – but for that you'd need to book well ahead, and there are far better places to eat for the price. *1200–1500 Mon–Fri, 1200–1600 Sun and 1900–0200 every day. Closed first two weeks of Aug.*

Virgin Café

Second Floor, Virgin Megastore, 52 Avenue des Champs-Élysées. Tel: 49 53 50 00. ££. If you don't want to pay sidewalk prices in the street outside, this is a good alternative, with views down onto the street, stylish décor, friendly staff, reasonable prices and a good range of dishes if you want a snack at lunchtime. Like most things British in Paris these days, this place has become a chic little hang-out. *1000–2400 Mon–Sat, 1200–2400 Sun, food all day.*

Bar des Théâtres

6 Avenue Montaigne. Tel: 47 23 34 63. £. A surprisingly inexpensive and decent café/bar/brasserie on the fashion-conscious Avenue Montaigne (*see page 155*). You may see models or fashion victims, designers or theatre-goers, in the light and bright café area – though there is a restaurant area too. *0600–0200 daily, hot food 1200–0200.*

Restaurants

Guy Savoy

18 Rue Troyon. Tel: 43 80 40 61. £££. If you have one blow-out to break the bank in Paris, this could be the place. The best of *haute cuisine* without the pomp of more old-fashioned places: they won't look shocked if you ask to share a dish between two. Expect dishes such as artichoke soup with parmesan and truffles, sea bass grilled in sweet spices, or veal with truffled potato purée. Also expect a bill of at least 1000F. *1200–1400 Mon–Fri, 1900–2230 Mon–Sat.*

Maxim's

3 Rue Royale. Tel: 42 65 27 94 £££. A temple of French dining, with orchestral music and loads of glitz. Cooking doesn't always match the price, and you may not even get in if you're not glam enough – but an experience nevertheless. *1230–1400 and 1930–2200 Mon–Sat, closed Mon in July and Aug.*

Maison de l'Alsace

39 Avenue des Champs-Élysées. Tel: 53 93 97 00. ££. A great place in among the tourist traps, it is open 24 hours, has a pavement seating area, and if you want more than a coffee or a snack, it serves good food from Alsace. A regional speciality is *baeckoeffe*, which is a meaty mixture of pork, veal, lamb and potatoes slowly roasted in the oven in wine – but so slowly that it has to be ordered 48 hours in advance. *24 hours daily.*

Le Boeuf sur le Toit

34 Rue du Colisée. Tel: 43 59 83 80. ££. Another good option in the Champs-Élysées area, where it's very easy to get an indifferent meal. This Art Deco place does a fixed-price dinner of oysters, steak and dessert, but the main menu is broader, with Mediterranean, regional and Asian choices. A reasonably-priced wine list makes this worth seeking out in an overpriced area. *1200–0200 daily.*

Chez Savy

23 Rue Bayard. Tel: 47 23 46 98. £–££. A sign that Parisian food is not generally over-priced is this excellent bistro not far from fashionable Avenue Montaigne, where you might expect prices to be much higher – you can get a modest fixed-price menu here for as little as 130F. Pay more and you'll get the best Auvergnat cooking, which tends to be meaty and hearty. A smart place with friendly service. *1200–1500 and 1900–2300 Mon–Fri.*

Les Ambassadeurs

Hôtel de Crillon, 10 Place de la Concorde. Tel: 44 71 16 16. £££. If you want to sample sheer Parisian style, then the dining room at Les Ambassadeurs will deliver it in spades. It's been called the best hotel restaurant in Paris, and new chef Dominique Bouchet takes over where his predecessor Christian Constant – who revolutionised the French restaurant scene – left off. Be prepared to pay through the nose (though there's a more affordable menu at lunchtime) but be prepared to be pampered and sample some of the best food in the city. *1200–1430 and 1900–2230 daily.*

159

Restorative *restaurant*

It is claimed that the first private restaurant in the world opened in Rue Bailleul, between the Louvre and Les Halles, in 1765. An innkeeper named Boulanger began serving cooked meals in his tavern, in defiance of a previous government monopoly on the provision of food to travellers. His main dish was sheep's meat in a white sauce, described as a restorative: a restaurante.

Clubs and nightlife

Lido

116 Avenue des Champs-Élysées. Tel: 40 76 56 00. The costumes alone for one of these spectacular shows are reckoned to cost over £2 million, and whether or not you like seeing topless dancers and mingling with Japanese tourists, the special effects are stunning. Less so the food. *Open 2000 for dinner, shows at 2200 and 2400, nightly.*

Montecristo Café

68 Rue des Champs-Élysées. Tel: 45 62 30 86. £££. If you're going to pay Champs-Élysées prices, then at least go somewhere with a bit of character, like this Cuban bar/restaurant – though drinks and music, maybe with some affordable tapas, is the best bet. Salsa and other Caribbean sounds from DJs on Fridays and Saturdays. *1100–0600 daily, food always available.*

Shopping

Virgin Records Megastore

52–60 Avenue des Champs-Élysées. Tel: 49 53 50 00. A vast selection of records on several floors, all of which you can hear instantly by waving them under the bar-code reader at the nearest headset. Software, too, plus bookstore, concert tickets and those hard-to-find French movies on video. A popular and pleasant café upstairs. *1000–2400 Mon–Sat, 1200–2400 Sun.*

Avenue Montaigne

See page 155.

Carrousel du Louvre

Tel: 43 16 47 47. This shopping complex beneath the inverted pyramid near the Louvre is a curious mix of the upmarket and downmarket, with bog-standard souvenir shops next door to smart boutiques, and in the middle is a huge fast-food eating hall where you can sample Asian, French, Mexican or other cuisines and take your tray to a table in the centre.

Androuët

41 Rue Arsène-Houssaye. Tel: 42 89 95 00. The best cheese shop in Paris, just off the top of the Champs-Élysées. Lovely interior with the bewildering array of hundreds of cheeses lined up temptingly on wooden shelves. Restaurant too. *1000–2000 Mon–Fri, 0900–2000 Sat.*

Photographers' Paris

*Paris has produced some great photographers who have chronicled the city every bit as well as its artists. **Brassaï** was a Hungarian photographer who settled in Paris and after recording conventional street scenes turned his lens on night-time Paris, gaining the trust of strippers, prostitutes and criminals, and producing unflinching portraits of their world.*

It is almost impossible to browse at a postcard stand without seeing the work of another great: **Robert Doisneau**. This French photographer trained in Paris and was greatly influenced by Brassaï. He developed his own style, however, and chronicled the quirky incidents in the life of the city: children in school, lovers in the street and amusing juxtapositions, such as a row of underpants on a washing line with the Eiffel Tower in the background.

Henri Cartier-Bresson

The greatest of them all, though, is **Henri Cartier-Bresson**, who was the first photographer to have a work exhibited at the Louvre. He still lives in Paris in his apartment overlooking the Seine, and after a lifetime of photography is now spending his time sketching and painting. His images linger on, though – lovers kissing in pavement cafés or by the banks of the Seine, gendarmes, the rows of trees in the Tuileries. He has captured Paris perfectly.

November is photography month

In even-numbered years (1998 was one), November is the Month of Photography in Paris. A booklet lists the hundreds of exhibitions and events in the city's galleries and museums, and even in private houses, cybercafés and other venues. Parisians take the art of photography seriously. Even if it is not the month of photography, there are bound to be exhibitions on somewhere, most notably at the **Maison Européenne de la Photographie** (*see page 99*). A second home to photography, though lagging behind the European gallery in terms of space and style, is the **Centre National de la Photographie** (*11 Rue Benyer; tel: 53 76 12 31; 1200–1900 Wed–Mon*).

163

Two other galleries show temporary exhibitions, so check what is on at the time of your visit. These are the **Espace Photographique de Paris** (*Nouveau Forum des Halles 4–8 Grand Galerie; tel: 40 26 87 12; usually open 1300–1800 Wed–Fri, 1300–1900 Sat–Sun*) and **La Mission du Patrimoine Photographique** (*62 Rue St-Antoine; tel: 42 74 47 75; usually open 1000–1830 Tue–Sun*).

Walks and excursions

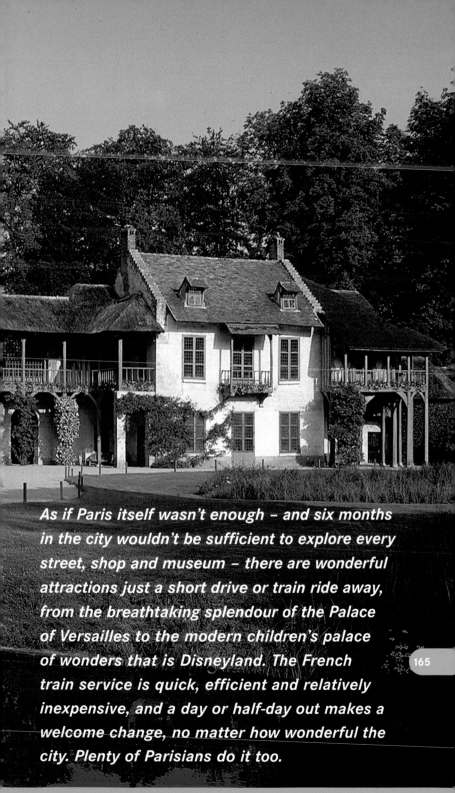

As if Paris itself wasn't enough – and six months in the city wouldn't be sufficient to explore every street, shop and museum – there are wonderful attractions just a short drive or train ride away, from the breathtaking splendour of the Palace of Versailles to the modern children's palace of wonders that is Disneyland. The French train service is quick, efficient and relatively inexpensive, and a day or half-day out makes a welcome change, no matter how wonderful the city. Plenty of Parisians do it too.

Versailles

A visit to the sumptuous Palace and Gardens of Versailles is probably the single most popular day trip from Paris, and is easily done by bus or using the RER train, the Palace being only 23km (14 miles) to the southwest of the city centre. Try to get there as early as possible, not just to beat the crowds but to allow the maximum time for your visit – there is a great deal to see, particularly in the vast gardens, which cover 250 acres. To give some impression of the scale, in the late 18th century the Palace was said to be home to no fewer than 20,000 servants.

The **Palace** was first built in 1624 in order to create a hunting lodge for King Louis XIII, but the buildings and grounds were expanded by Louis XIV until eventually Versailles was made the capital of France. As you enter the main gate and cross the vast expanse of the Ministers' Courtyard, you will instantly realise that you are never going to see more than a small percentage of the buildings and grounds. Beyond this first courtyard is the Royal Courtyard, and beyond that the Marble Courtyard, overlooked by a clock with the Sun King emblem in the centre.

The Court of the Sun King

The Sun King was Louis XIV (1638–1715), who was king of France from 1643 until 1715, making him the longest reigning monarch in Europe. It was in 1668 that he first started work on transforming his father's hunting lodge into the largest palace in Europe. One of his first requests was for a private pavilion where he could take his mistresses, and this was provided in the form of the Trianon de Porcelaine. In 1687 this was replaced by the **Grand Trianon**, a marble structure that still stands in the grounds. Not far away is the **Petit Trianon**, which was added by Louis XV in 1762 but is better known for its associations with Marie Antoinette, who loved it and spent a great deal of time there.

Other highlights in the gardens include the Grand Canal, where royal boating parties used to be held and where today you can hire bicycles to make it easier to negotiate the grounds, the Water Parterres immediately behind the Palace with their ornate bronze statues, and the nearby **Orangerie**, where the hot-house plants were kept.

Mirrors to the world

For security reasons only sections of the Palace are completely open to the public – mainly the State Apartments and the **Hall of Mirrors (Galerie des Glaces)**. The latter was built in 1687 and was intended to be the most impressive room in the whole Palace, where overseas guests could be welcomed to show off the Sun King's wealth, and where

court entertainments could be held. The Hall is 75m (246ft) long and 12m (40ft) high, with 17 windows facing 17 mirrors, each of which is made up of 34 separate pieces of glass – the largest pieces that were capable of being made at that time.

Other areas of the Palace can be seen by taking a guided tour, which you are advised to book in advance at busy times of the year.

INFORMATION

Distance:	23km (14 miles) southwest of Paris.
By train:	take the RER, line C, to Versailles-Rive Gauche, then a short walk through the town to the Château.
By car:	take the A13 from the Porte d'Auteuil, or the N10 from the Porte de Sèvres.
Tourist information:	7 Rue des Réservoirs. Tel: 01 39 50 36 22. 0900–1900 daily May–Oct, 0900–1230 and 1330–1800 Mon–Sat Nov–Apr.

Fontainebleau

*The **Forêt de Fontainebleau** spreads over 96 square miles and is one of the most impressive areas of woodland within fairly easy reach of central Paris – it's about 65km (40 miles) southeast of the city. If you like the outdoors, then there is something here for everyone, and you're likely to find groups of birdwatchers or mushroom-pickers, depending on the season, as well as walkers, cyclists, picnickers and horse-riders.*

Unusual rock formations bring rock climbers long distances to practise their skills here. There are miles of marked trails, with a map of them available from the tourist office in the town, and cycles available for hire too (*see pages 14–15 and 169 for information*). Alternatively, buy a copy of the Michelin map number 196 (Environs de Paris), which also marks the forest trails.

Fontainebleau Palace

The **Château de Fontainebleau** (*tel: 01 60 71 50 70; 0930–1800 Wed–Mon July–Aug, 0930–1700 Wed–Mon May–June/Sept–Oct, 0930–1230, and 1400–1700 Wed–Mon Nov–Apr*) was established here because the forest was the perfect place for royal hunting expeditions. An abbey was originally on the site, consecrated by Thomas à Beckett in 1169, but this was later replaced by a hunting lodge. Then in the early 16th century the lodge was transformed into the most sumptuous Italian palace in the whole of France, and Italian architects, artists and artisans were brought here to work on it. This initial work was done by François I, but later kings were so enamoured of the place that they also lavished attention on it, each adding his own distinctive style, which ultimately created the glorious mix of architecture that is now part of its appeal.

> *Despite its name – an antique contraction of* fontaine de belle eau – *the forest is all but waterless, a desert out of which pines, oaks, beeches and wild cherry trees somehow connive to spring. Aeons flooded the plain with limestone; millennial rains wore this softer stuff away, leaving woods strewn with grotesque sandstone monuments up to 50 feet high. The homely taxonomy of English calls such an assemblage a 'boulder pile'; in French, it forms a chaos.*

David Roberts, 'Bonjour, Chaos'

Henri IV added two courtyards and a tennis court to the Château, and one of its most striking features was added by Louis XIII: a horseshoe-shaped staircase which leads up to the house while allowing carriages to pass beneath and on into the interior courtyard. Louis XIV, Louis XV and Napoléon also all added their own flourishes. Napoléon's apartments, which were added to the rear of the building and which must not be missed, contain his suitably Napoleonic throne, while the Galerie François I contains much of the work created by the original Italian artists and craftsmen. There are also the gardens to enjoy, including the Jardin Anglais and the Jardin de Diane.

Barbizon and the arts

A few miles from the Château is the tiny village of **Barbizon**, which art lovers will certainly want to see. The forests and landscapes around have attracted artists since Corot first moved there in 1830, followed by other artists in the 1840s, most notably Rousseau, Daubigny and Millet. Rousseau's studio in the Auberge Ganne is now a museum to what became known as the Barbizon School, whose work is also on display in Musée d'Orsay (*see pages 40–41*).

INFORMATION

Distance:	60km (36 miles) southeast of Paris.
By train:	from Gare de Lyon to Fontainebleau-Avon, journey time 50 minutes, then bus direct to Château.
By car:	take the A6 to the Fontainebleau exit, then the N7.
Tourist information:	4 Rue Royale. Tel: 01 60 74 99 99. 0930–1830 Mon–Sat, 1000–1230 and 1500–1730 Sun June–Sept; 0930–1730 Sun–Fri, 1000–1800 Sat, Oct–May.

169

Disneyland Paris

*It is quite easy to have a break from Parisian culture and spend a day sampling Disney culture instead, at **Disneyland Paris**. The Magic Kingdom is only 32km (20 miles) east of Paris in Marne-la-Vallée, linked by the RER train line (see pages 14–15 for further information).*

The amusement park opened in 1992, transforming a 4,806-acre site into an approximate replica of Disney's other sites in California, Florida and Japan, and incorporating six hotels, a campsite, apartments, 29 restaurants and a golf course. Expansion means there are now 40 restaurants inside, with a picnic area outside (no 'non-Disney' food is allowed inside Disneyland).

Queues, queues and queues

Like those other parks, Disneyland Paris (sometimes still referred to by its now-dropped original name of Euro Disneyland) is divided up into five areas: Main Street USA, Adventureland, Discoveryland, Fantasyland and Frontierland. And just as with the Louvre, a little advance planning will improve your visit considerably. Check train times and current opening times, and arrive there when they open the doors, if at all possible. Queues build up quickly, just as they do in the art galleries. This time, however, there are queues inside too for each and every attraction – though at least there are signs indicating how long you might expect to wait according to the length of the queue (more than you get when you're trying to get near the *Mona Lisa*). Take careful note of these signs, as rides like Small World can take a lot of people on each trip, so a long queue doesn't always mean a long wait.

Rides for big and small

If you have toddlers with you, then head for Fantasyland first, as this includes many of the simpler rides such as Small World which seem to appeal to them most. In fact they appeal so much that you may need to pack an extra dose of patience with you. Older children will want the big-thrills rides, and these are divided up among Adventureland, Discoveryland and Frontierland.

If you do get to Disneyland early, head for Space Mountain, which is by far the fastest ride in the park, and a thrilling experience as you hurtle through pitch darkness at speeds of up to 75k/h (47mph). For those that don't make the entry requirements – 1.4m (4ft 3in) tall or over ten years old – there's an entrance round the back where you can watch the ride. Other 'white-knuckle' rides include Indiana Jones and the Temple of Doom (Temple du Péril in French), for which you have to be 1.4m (4ft 3in) tall or eight years old, and Big Thunder Mountain (1.02m/3ft 1in tall or three years old).

Other star rides include Pirates of the Caribbean and Haunted Mansion, both of which appeal to all age groups. Children will just sit and wonder, while adults will wonder how it's done. Leave Main Street USA until you're leaving, as this is mostly where the souvenir shops are, and you don't want to waste time looking round those while other people are heading for the rides.

INFORMATION

Distance:	32km (20 miles) east of Paris.
By train:	RER, line A, to Marne-la-Vallée.
By car:	A4 to exit 14, then follow signs to Disneyland.
Tourist information:	Tel: 01 60 30 60 30; 0900–2300 daily July–Sept, 1000–1800 Sun–Fri and 1000–2000 Sat Oct–June, but check as exact seasonal opening times vary.

Giverny

The father of Impressionism, Claude Monet, lived at **Giverny** *from 1883, when he moved in with one mistress and eight children, until he died at the age of 86 in 1926. If you have seen any of his Impressionist paintings of the gardens – most notably the many vivid water-lily paintings, especially the ones normally on display at the Orangerie in the Jardin des Tuileries (see page 151) – then you will recognise what it was that gave him his inspiration.*

The house and four acres of grounds were rather neglected until Michel Monet, Claude's son, donated them to the Académie des Beaux-Arts in 1966, and then in 1977, with grass still growing in the artist's former studio, work was begun to restore them to their former glory. At last they can be appreciated just as they were in Monet's day. The only drawback is that they can no longer offer the peace and seclusion which Monet found here, as the house and grounds are invariably busy – but that should not put anyone off a visit as they are also invariably beautiful.

The seasons at Giverny

Spring and early summer are probably the best times, when the colours are showing but before too many crowds are showing too. Autumn also sees the gardens looking gorgeous, and crowds start to tail off after the summer season, but remember that the house is not open all year round (though the gardens are).

The house in which Monet lived, charmingly built of pink bricks and now decorated in the artist's favourite colours, is open to visitors and a gift shop sells good-quality prints, postcards and even plates and cups which were designed by Monet. None of his original paintings are here, which is understandable given their value and the security problems that this would generate.

It is the gardens, though, which make the main attraction. There are two: the Normandy Garden by the house and the Japanese Water Garden, which is connected to it by an underground tunnel and contains most of the familiar sights: lilies, bridges, ponds, willow trees. In fact, Monet's friends sometimes said to him that his greatest work of art was the very gardens that he created.

Along the road from the gardens a museum has been opened which highlights the work of several American artists who came to the town in the wake of Monet, and here there are original paintings on display. The **Musée Americain** (*99 Rue Claude-Monet; tel: 02 32 51 94 65; 1000–1800 Tue–Sun Apr–Oct*) has a very pleasant tea room, which is good and tends to be quieter than Giverny itself.

INFORMATION

Distance:	80km (48 miles) west of Paris.
By train:	from Gare St-Lazare, 45 minutes to Vernon station, then taxi/bus for 5km (3 miles) to Giverny.
By car:	A13 from the Porte d'Auteuil to Bonnières, then the D201 to Giverny.
Tourist information:	Tel: 02 32 51 28 21; 1000–1800 Tue–Sun Apr–Oct.

Lifestyles

Shopping, eating, children and nightlife in Paris

Shopping

This is the city that gave the world its first 'flea market' – or at least that phrase – and though it's not exactly the kind of city you come to in the hope of hunting down bargains, shopping – if only window-shopping – is one of its major delights.

Gourmet goods

Food comes high on anyone's shopping list, whether it be simply good, fresh produce bought in one of the markets to take home or eat as a

picnic lunch, or the most mouth-watering chocolates and patisseries in shop windows where the very displays are works of art. There are markets every day of the week in Paris, though many take a break on Sunday afternoons and Mondays. Anyone who can walk down the stalls of a typical street market and fail to want to fill a shopping bag doesn't have eyes to see or a nose to smell. Even if you genuinely don't want to buy, take a look anyway at the best goods that France – and the seas around it – can provide: oysters, mushrooms, cheeses, wines, bread, rainbows of fruit and vegetables.

Fashionable Paris

Alongside food, **fashion** is naturally the other good buy in Paris, even if it's only a wish-purchase. In no other city in the world will you have chance to see so many designer clothes for sale in the same place, from cool Kenzo to flamboyant Gaultier and Christian Lacroix. You might think the real top stuff is out of your price bracket but you can find some bargains especially in the shops that sell second-hand designer goods, which have frequently been worn only once for some special event (*see page 127*).

Some of the more distinctive shops are in the **passages**, the arcaded galleries that surround or run through elegant 19th-century buildings, mainly in the 2nd and 9th *arrondissements*, including the Galerie Vivienne and Galerie Colbert off Rue Vivienne, the Passage des Panoramas (the oldest, dating from about 1800) and the *passages* of the

Palais Royal off Rue de Montpensier. These often provide small shops, ideal for the specialist trader, and you're likely to find hat designers, toy shops, leather specialists, antiquarian bookshops and often with characterful little cafés too.

Department stores

Don't ignore the big department stores either. They may more resemble the kinds of stores you can find back home, such as John Lewis, but they are frequently on a vast scale, and one of the biggest, **Galeries Lafayette** (*40 Boulevard Haussmann; tel: 42 82 34 56*), has been described as the 'Louvre of department stores'. In one month, the equivalent of the entire population of Paris walks through its doors, and inside you can find flash fashion like Vivienne Westwood, more affordable alternatives such as Gap and agnès b, a floor devoted to lingerie, another to children's wear, enough shoes to supply an army, cooking utensils you never knew existed and two restaurants.

Along the street from Galeries Lafayette is **Le Printemps** (*64 Boulevard Haussmann; tel: 42 82 50 00*), the other huge department store, which is actually three stores in one, with one devoted to women's fashions, one to men's and another to items for the home. The women's shop now has the biggest accessories department in Paris, and you can buy names like Dior, Chanel, Alexander McQueen and Dolce e Gabbana.

Male travellers may prefer to mooch around in **BHV** (*52–64 Rue de Rivoli; tel: 42 74 90 00*), which is DIY heaven, stocking more hardware items than you ever knew existed. It's so big there's a Visitor Welcome Centre on the ground floor to help you find what you're looking for, though half the fun is in browsing. At a recent count the store estimated it had 350,000 DIY items.

Opening times

From a practical point of view, shops often close on a Monday as well as Sunday, although lots of food shops do open for business on a Sunday morning, especially where there is a local market that brings shoppers in. If you happen to be travelling back home on a Sunday, don't feel you have to buy foodstuffs the day before. You will have plenty of choice on the Sunday morning, so do your clothes shopping on a Saturday. Note also that many shops and stores stay open into the evenings, and some have one night a week of **late opening** in midweek. Galeries Lafayette, for example, stays open until 2100 on a Thursday, while BHV is open until 2200 on a Wednesday.

Eating out

It seems to have become an accepted fact that Paris is an expensive place in which to eat and drink. True, it can be, and you will have no shortage of restaurants to choose from if you want to spend £100 and more on a meal. You can also easily spend £5 on a cup of coffee, if you choose to sit in a prime location like a pavement café on the Champs-Élysées. The consolation will be that the food will probably be terrific, and the coffee better than you would get if you could even find a pavement café with as good a location in London.

However, Paris on average is not so expensive as people like to make out. You can just as easily find yourself a restaurant where you could have a five-course meal for less than £20, and it would be food of a standard that would cost twice as much in most other European capital cities. One way to keep costs down without spoiling the fun of eating out is to stick to the fixed-price menus. Many places offer a range of these to suit different budgets, and most places will have at least one *prix fixe* menu featuring the dish of the day, or *plat du jour*. Fixed-price menus generally offer three courses, or sometimes any two courses from three listed, at the price stated. This won't include wine but note that menu prices in Paris are bound by law to include a service charge of 12–15 per cent, so there should be no extra mark-up. If you wish to leave an extra little tip as an appreciation of particularly good service then that is entirely up to you, but the price quoted for a *prix fixe* meal is exactly what you should pay, save for the cost of drinks. Do read the small print on the menu before choosing what you are going to have, as sometimes the best fixed-price bargains are only available in the restaurant equivalent of a 'happy hour', ie outside the main eating times.

Opening hours

Parisians tend to eat late, although not as late as the Spaniards. Lunch will begin at about 1300–1330, as Paris is a working city with no tradition of siesta, and the lengthy expense-account lunch, if not dead, is certainly on the danger list in today's economic climate. Restaurants will generally be open in the evenings by 1900–1930, but early diners are more likely to be visitors than locals. Parisians prefer to eat no earlier than 2000, and frequently much later.

Booking

If you want to dine in a particularly good restaurant but haven't booked a few weeks ahead, then you might be able to get a table if you are prepared to turn up at opening time. Many places listed in this guide do require booking, some several weeks in advance, especially for the busy nights of Friday and Saturday. If you have booked your holiday, don't trust to luck but pick up the phone and reserve a table. Most places are used to English-speaking visitors, whether they be British, American or Japanese, so even if your French is rusty you should be able to book a table. The standard of food in the best places is worth a little effort.

“ *'Let's search the Left Bank,' I proposed to a friend, 'Let's try to find a bad meal.'*

We succeeded. It was in an Algerian restaurant on the rue Xavier Privas, because we wanted couscous, that North African specialty of grains and vegetables and spices and various meats. But we cheated: it was a restaurant aimed like a missile at tourists, with a barker outside; and even here the food was merely mediocre, perhaps even interesting, which of course is not a word of highest commendation for food. One can eat poorly only with the greatest difficulty in the myriad of small restaurants of the Rive Gauche. ”

Herbert Gold, 'On the Left Bank'

Paris with children

Although it is primarily seen as the ultimate romantic destination for couples, Paris has more than enough options for children to make it a good place for a family holiday too. Don't force the kids to spend too much time in the major adult attractions, such as the Louvre or the Musée d'Orsay, and everyone should be happy.

Several museums have equal appeal to adults and children, though parents will have to be prepared to do a certain amount of translating. The features that attract the youngsters, such as computer displays and films, are frequently in French only. On the other hand, if they are learning French at school, it could be that they do the translating for you.

One of the best options is the excellent multimedia **Galerie de l'Évolution** in the Jardin des Plantes (*see pages 64–65*). Extensive use of touch-screen computers, videos and sound effects, as well as the actual exhibits themselves, should appeal to children of all ages. Outside, the Jardin also has a playground, a small zoo and of course lots of room for running around.

Hands-on science

Even better, although further from the centre, is the **Cité des Sciences** in the Parc de la Villette. Among the many exciting interactive exhibits are a planetarium, a weather station, and the chance to try landing a plane or watch a nuclear explosion. There are even two special sections, for younger and older children, called the **Cité des Enfants**. Also in the Parc are playgrounds, a cinema, a submarine and a flight simulator. *Parc and museum open daily except Mon (Métro: Porte de la Villette).*

The **Musée de l'Homme** in the Palais de Chaillot (*see page 25*) is another museum where thought has been given to appealing to children, and across the river the **Eiffel Tower** (*see pages 22–23*) has to be the ultimate children's treat.

Sewers and skeletons

Anything grimy or ghoulish appeals to children, so take them on a visit to the **sewers** (*see pages 34–35*) or to see the **Catacombs**, which contain a few million skeletons. Take a torch to explore 'the empire of the dead'. The Catacombs are beneath Place Denfert-Rochereau in Montparnasse. *Open weekday afternoons, and weekend mornings and afternoons. Métro: Denfert-Rochereau.*

Simply **travelling** around the city should provide some entertainment for children. Let them use the tickets and plan the route – some of the bigger stations have computer displays, which will provide you with suggested routes to your destination. A boat on the river provides a distraction for children and a chance for parents to get a different view of Paris's architecture.

While **theatres** and **cinemas** are of limited interest unless your children have good French (films, including cartoons, are almost invariably dubbed into French rather than subtitled), there are plenty of circuses in Paris. In France the **circus** is regarded as an art form, and your children – like the French themselves – will probably have no qualms about seeing animals performing in them. Get a copy of *Pariscope* magazine for a list of current performance days and times.

 France may be Paris, but Paris is not France. **99**

Henry James,
***A Little Tour of France* (1884)**

181

After dark

*Paris starts to light up when the lights go down. Some visitors want to see a show, like the Crazy Horse or the Moulin Rouge (see **Naked Paris** pages 140–141), and others want to join the Parisians in eating their way through the evening. Eat out and you're reminded how Paris, like many cities, is a collection of villages: diners often know each other, or know the patron, or go out to eat in a group to make the whole event a much more sociable occasion that lasts till late. The night doesn't stop there, though, as then it's on to a bar or a club, where closing time will be the early hours – early hours if you're working next day, but also still early hours for the dedicated clubbers, who will be out till dawn – a convenient time to finish when the Métro starts up again at 0530.*

The club and disco scene in Paris is pretty vibrant, influenced as it is by the music of African immigrants, feeding off the long association the city has with jazz, especially black musicians (*see pages 70–71*). Rap thrives here. Brit chic also reaches all levels, from those who like to shop at Marks and Spencer to those who keep in close touch with the London club and house scene, and bring the music back with them.

From can-can to karaoke

Paris has always had a buoyant cabaret scene, whether it be the super-spectaculars of the Lido, which would cease to exist without the tourist francs to keep them going, or the more localised cabaret-clubs, the tradition of *chansons*,

of satirical comedy and verse, the *cafés-concerts*. On the import side, karaoke bars are just as popular here as everywhere else in the world, so while the Parisians are enjoying the Japanese 'tradition' of karaoke, the Japanese are all at the Moulin Rouge watching the can-can dancers. The best place to find out about anything happening in Paris at night is a listings magazine like *Pariscope*, which has a special *Paris la nuit* section, covering everything from *thés dansants* to *spectacles érotiques*.

On the night boat

When Paris is lit up at night, it looks every bit as beautiful as it does during

the day. The pyramid at the Louvre glows, as do the honey-coloured walls of the palace around it. Across the river the mighty Notre-Dame glowers down, while the visitors go sailing by enjoying a night-time boat tour on the *bateaux-mouches*. In many

cities this might seem corny, but Paris is so incredibly beautiful at night, especially when viewed slowly from the Seine, that an evening boat trip is a visual treat. The food may even surprise you too, once you've let the first glass of champagne put you into a mellow mood.

Licensing laws

The French drink more alcohol than anyone else in the world, but you won't see too many drunks, as the drinking is social and spread over a lunch and/or a dinner. They don't binge on the booze. There are no universal licensing hours, as each establishment applies for its own licence and hours. Some may stop serving drinks and close as early as 2200, others at 0200, and others have round-the-clock licences.

Practical information

PRACTICAL INFORMATION

Practical information

Airport

The main airport is Roissy–Charles de Gaulle (*tel: 48 62 22 80*), to the northeast of the city, which is used by both BA and Air France. There are several options for getting into the city, the cheapest being the Roissy bus, which leaves every 15 minutes (*0600–2300*) and takes 45 minutes to reach Opéra-Garnier by Place de l'Opéra, near which are stations for several different Métro lines. Air France buses run every 15 minutes (*0545–2300*) and stop in several places. including Avenue Carnot off the Arc de Triomphe. The quickest transfer is on the Roissy-Rail, which takes just over 30 minutes but involves using the airport bus and the RER train to Gare du Nord or the Les Halles/Châtelet RER and Métro complex. Taxis should cost roughly 200–300 francs, depending on destination and traffic.

Climate

Paris is similar to London though has more rainfall. Midsummer sees temperatures into the upper 20s°C (80s°F) but with August being the Parisian month for holidays it is not a good time to visit as many places close down. Late spring and early autumn are ideal times, as the average January temperature is only 3°C (38°F).

Currency

The French franc, written as FFr, FF or sometimes just F, is divided into 100 centimes. Notes are in denominations of 500, 200, 100, 50, 20 and 10 francs. Coins are in denominations of 10, 5, 2 francs and 1 franc, and 50, 20, 10 and 5 centimes.

Customs regulations

The following goods may be imported into France without incurring customs duty by:

(a) Passengers over 17 years of age entering from countries outside the EU: 200 cigarettes or 50 cigars or 100 cigarillos or 250g of tobacco; 1 litre of spirits or 2 litres of alcoholic beverage up to 22%; 2 litres of wine; 60g of perfume and 250ml of eau-de-toilette; other goods to the value of 300 francs (150 francs per person under 15 years of age).

(b) Passengers over 17 years of age entering from an EU country: 300 cigarettes or 75 cigars or 150 cigarillos or 400g of tobacco; 1.5 litres of spirits of more than 22% or 3 litres of spirits or sparkling wine up to 22%; 5 litres of wine; 75g of perfume and 375ml of eau-de-toilette; other goods to the value of 4200 francs (1100 francs per person under 15 years of age).

(c) Passengers over 17 years of age entering from an EU country with duty-paid goods: 800 cigarettes or 400 cigarillos or 200 cigars or 1kg of tobacco; 90 litres of wine (including up to 60 litres of sparkling wine); 10 litres of spirits; 20 litres of intermediate products (such as fortified wine); 110 litres of beer.

Prohibited items: Gold objects, other than personal jewellery below 500g in weight.

Disabled travellers

Many of the newer museums in Paris have been designed with the disabled visitor in mind, and although access is not always easy in other places, the city is well-stocked with information. There are several guides which you should be able to obtain from the French Government Tourist Office in London, or from their main office in Paris on the Champs-Élysées, covering hotels, museums and cinemas/theatres. There is also *Access in Paris* by Gordon Couch and Ben Roberts (Quiller Press). The Métro is not well suited to wheelchair users, though a Braille map for the blind is available from L'Association Valentin Haüy (*5 Rue Duroc, Paris 75007; tel: 47 34 07 90*). However, RER lines A and B have access for wheelchairs, and taxi drivers are legally obliged to take disabled passengers and help them into the vehicle. Generally people are willing to help even if the facilities are not always there.

Electricity

The French electricity supply is 220V – sufficient to work with 240V British appliances. The plugs have two pins, which are large for heavy-duty items and small for the small devices most visitors are likely to bring with them, so an adapter will be needed. If you forget to pack one, French hardware stores stock them.

Entry formalities

British citizens do not require a visa, but those who have retained their Commonwealth passports may need one. Check with the visa section of the Consulate for details.

Health

No vaccinations are needed. Rabies is present in France and there are lots of dogs in Paris, but very few of them are strays so a rabies jab is probably not necessary.

Information

Maison de la France (Tourist Information Agency) *8 Avenue de l'Opéra, 75001 Paris, France. Tel: (01) 42 96 10 23. Fax: (01) 42 86 80 52.*

Direction du Tourisme *2 Rue Linois, 75740 Paris, Cedex 15, France. Tel: (01) 44 37 37 44. Fax: (01) 44 37 38 39.*

Embassy of the French Republic *58 Knightsbridge, London SW1X 7JT. Tel: 0171–201 1000. Fax: 0171–201 1004.*

French Consulate General (Visa Section) *PO Box 57, 6A Cromwell Place, London SW7 2EW. Tel: 0171–838 2000. Information Service: 0891 887733 (calls charged at 39p/49p per minute). Fax: 0171–838 2046. Open 0900–1130 (and 1600–1630 for visa collection only) Mon–Fri (except French and British national holidays).*

Consulate in Scotland *Tel: 0131– 225 7954. Fax: 0131–225 8975.*

French Embassy (Cultural Section) *23 Cromwell Road, London SW7 2EL. Tel: 0171–838 2055. Fax: 0171–838 2088. Open 0930–1300 and 1430–1700 Mon–Fri.*

French Government Tourist Office *78 Piccadilly, London W1V 0AL. Tel: 0891 244123 (France Information Line; calls charged at 39p/49p per minute). Fax: 0171–493 6594. Open 0900–1700 Mon–Fri.*

British Embassy *35 Rue du Faubourg St–Honoré, 75383 Paris, Cedex 08, France. Tel: (01) 42 66 91 42. Fax: (01) 42 66 95 90.*

Insurance

There is a reciprocal health agreement with the UK, so you should obtain a Form E111 from the Post Office before you go. On presentation of this at an office of the Caisse Primaire d'Assurance Maladies (Sickness Insurance Office), UK citizens are entitled to a refund of 70–80 per cent on dental and medical treatments, and on prescribed medicines. The standard of medical facilities in France is very high but so are the fees, and health insurance is recommended: a lot of paperwork is involved in obtaining refunds.

Maps

Free street maps are available from French tourist offices and from Métro stations. If you feel you need a more detailed street map then *The Paris Mapguide* by Michael Middleditch (Penguin, £4.99) is an excellent and almost pocket-sized choice.

Opening times

Shops: Department stores are open 0900–1830 Mon–Sat. Most shops are closed 1200–1430. Food shops are open 0700–1830/1930. Some food shops such as bakers and patisseries are open Sunday mornings, in which case they will probably close on Monday. Many shops close all day or half-day Monday.

Banks: Banks are generally open 0900–1200 and 1400–1600 Mon–Fri. Some banks close on Monday. Banks close at about noon on the day before a bank holiday.

Tourist offices: The main tourist office is at 127 Avenue des Champs-Élysées, just down from the Arc de Triomphe (*tel: 49 52 53 54; fax: 49 52 53 00*) and is open 0900–2000 daily except 1 Jan, 1 May and 25 Dec.

Businesses: Offices are generally open 0900–1200 and 1400–1800 Mon–Fri.

Bars and restaurants: These vary enormously depending on the proprietor. Some bars/cafés open early morning and stay open until the early hours of the next day. Restaurants generally open about 1200–1500, though some open and close a little later. Evening openings start at about 1900/1930 through to about 2200 for last orders. Many restaurants close on a Sunday.

Churches: Churches are generally open from dawn until dusk, but as is happening elsewhere in the world, many are increasingly being locked for security reasons.

Museums: Museums are usually open about 0900–1800, and closed on either Monday or Tuesday. Reduced or free admission is often available on Sunday. Many museums stay open late one evening in midweek, so check each museum for details.

Public holidays

1 Jan, Easter Sunday, Easter Monday, Feast of the Ascension (40 days after Easter), Whit Sunday (7th Sunday after Easter), Whit Monday, 1 May, 8 May (VE Day), 14 July (Bastille Day), 15 Aug (Feast of the Assumption), 1 Nov (All Saints), 11 Nov (Armistice Day), 25 Dec.

Reading

No one should visit Paris without reading Ernest Hemingway's classic evocation of his years there, *A Moveable Feast*. Even if his Paris of the 1920s has disappeared, it gives a very impressionistic account of a particular period which still resonates. George Orwell's *Down and Out in Paris and London* may also describe past times

66 *·And even if I don't live forever, which is always a possibility, Paris surely will.* 99

Herbert Gold, 'On the Left Bank'

but is a reminder of what goes on 'below stairs'. *Citizens* by Simon Schama brings the French Revolution vividly to life. *The Hunchback of Notre Dame* by Victor Hugo may be fiction but

visitors to the great cathedral will still want to read it. *Nana* by Émile Zola is both a social document and a novel that portrays the reality of sleazy/sexy Paris. Any Maigret novel by Georges Simenon provides background atmosphere. Theodore Zeldin's *The French* is a modern examination of both the country and its capital city, as is *On the Brink* by Jonathan Fenby.

Safety and Security

Paris is no more dangerous than any other European capital, and even beggars may well have the typical French politeness. Care needs to be taken in crowded places, as pickpockets are a particular problem, so keep your valuables close to you at all times.

Telephones

To ring Paris from the UK, dial 00 then 33 and omit the first zero of the number. To call the UK from Paris dial 00 then 44 and omit the first zero. The Paris city code is 01, which has been omitted from the numbers printed in this book. The majority of telephones are now card-only, the pre-paid cards being available from post offices or *tabacs*. International calls are cheaper 2230–0800 Mon–Fri, and from 1400 Sat to 0800 Mon.

Time

Paris is one hour ahead of Greenwich Mean Time and uses the 24-hour clock.

Tipping

Tip taxi drivers 10–20 per cent by rounding up the bill, and although tipping hotel staff such as chambermaids is not expected, a small appreciation of good service won't go amiss. In restaurants service is normally included and indicated on the bill (*service compris*), with 15 per cent being the usual rate. Again, extra good service might be rewarded with an additional small tip. It's not too long ago that French waiters were not actually paid and so relied on tips to make their living. This is no longer the case, but wages are still not high, so if you have a particularly professional waiter or waitress, reward them.

Toilets

A few years ago the phrase 'a French toilet' would have summoned up the idea of a hole in the ground and poor hygiene, but no more. French toilets are as good as any others in Europe, although the 'unisex' principal is stronger and even in Paris you must be prepared to find a row of cubicles used by both men and women. More common is a split loo, where you pass the attendant and go left or right, but be prepared to put a franc or two in the saucer when you leave.

Index

must-see PARIS

Editorial, design and production credits

Project management: Dial House Publishing Services

Series editor: Christopher Catling

Copy editor: Andrew Shakleton

Proof-reader: Posy Gosling

Series and cover design: Trickett & Webb Limited

Cover artwork: Wenham Arts

Text layout: Wenham Arts

Map work: RJS Associates

Repro and image setting: Z2 Repro, Thetford, Norfolk, UK

Printed and bound by: Artes Graficas ELKAR S. Coop., Bilbao, Spain

We would like to thank the following photographers and organisations for the
photographs used in this book, to whom the copyright in the photograph belongs:

Pages 34 and 35: Ann Ronan Picture Library

Pages 40 and 141: Jacques Lebar

Pages 51, 126 and 127: Rex Features

Page 100: Jean-Pierre Lescourret

Page 140: D'Herouville

Page 164: Michel Dusart

Page 167: Michel Beaugeois

Page 171: Guillaume de Laubier

All remaining pictures: Chris Fairclough

Picture research: Image Select International